Introduction to Communication

Grades 6–8

Susan O'Connell
Suzanne G. Croskey

The Math Process Standards Series
Susan O'Connell, Series Editor

HEINEMANN
Portsmouth, NH

Heinemann
361 Hanover Street
Portsmouth, NH 03801–3912
www.heinemann.com

Offices and agents throughout the world

The authors and publisher wish to thank those who have generously given permission to reprint borrowed material:

Excerpts from *Principles and Standards for School Mathematics*. Copyright © 2000 by the National Council of Teachers of Mathematics. Reprinted with permission. All rights reserved.

Library of Congress Cataloging-in-Publication Data
O'Connell, Susan.
    Introduction to communication : grades 6–8 / Susan O'Connell, Suzanne G. Croskey.
        p. cm. — (The math process standards series)
    Includes bibliographical references.
    ISBN-13: 978-0-325-01732-7
    ISBN-10: 0-325-01732-8
    1. Mathematics—Study and teaching (Secondary).   2. Mathematics—Study and teaching (Secondary)—Activity programs.   3. Mathematics—Language.
I. Croskey, Suzanne G.   II. Title.
    QA135.6.O2873 2008
    510.71′2—dc22   2007044325

Editor: Emily Michie Birch
Production coordinator: Elizabeth Valway
Production service: Matrix Productions Inc.
Cover design: Night & Day Design
Cover photography: Joy Bronston Schackow
Composition: Publishers' Design and Production Services, Inc.
CD production: Nicole Russell
Manufacturing: Louise Richardson

Printed in the United States of America on acid-free paper
12 11 10 09 08   ML   1 2 3 4 5

CONTENTS

_____

💿 *On the CD-ROM*

In order to be effective mathematicians, students need to develop understanding of critical math content. They need to understand number and operations, algebra, measurement, geometry, and data analysis and probability. Through continued study of these content domains, students gain a comprehensive understanding of mathematics as a subject with varied and interconnected concepts. As math teachers, we attempt to provide students with exposure to, exploration in, and reflection about the many skills and concepts that make up the study of mathematics.

Even with a deep understanding of math content, however, students may lack important skills that can assist them in their development as effective mathematicians. Along with content knowledge, students need an understanding of the processes used by mathematicians. They must learn to problem solve, communicate their ideas, reason through math situations, prove their conjectures, make connections between and among math concepts, and represent their mathematical thinking. Development of content alone does not provide students with the means to explore, express, or apply that content. As we strive to develop effective mathematicians, we are challenged to develop both students' content understanding and process skills.

The National Council of Teachers of Mathematics (2000) has outlined critical content and process standards in its *Principles and Standards for School Mathematics* document. These standards have become the roadmap for the development of textbooks, curriculum materials, and student assessments. These standards have provided a framework for thinking about what needs to be taught in math classrooms and how various skills and concepts can be blended together to create a seamless math curriculum. The first five standards outline content standards and expectations related to number and operations, algebra, geometry, measurement, and data analysis and probability. The second five standards outline the process goals of problem solving, reasoning and proof, communication, connections, and representations. A strong understanding of these standards empowers teachers to identify and select activities within their curricula to produce powerful learning. The standards provide a vision for what teachers hope their students will achieve.

This book is a part of a vital series designed to assist teachers in understanding the NCTM Process Standards and the ways in which they impact and guide student learning. An additional goal of this series is to provide practical ideas to support teachers as they ensure that the acquisition of process skills has a critical place in their math instruction. Through this series, teachers will gain an understanding of each process standard as well as gather ideas for bringing that standard to life within their math classrooms. It offers practical ideas for lesson development, implementation, and assessment that work with any curriculum. Each book in the series focuses on a critical process skill in a highlighted grade band and all books are designed to encourage reflection about teaching and learning. The series also highlights the interconnected nature of the process and content standards by showing correlations between them and showcasing activities that address multiple standards.

Students who develop an understanding of content skills and cultivate the process skills that allow them to apply that content understanding become effective mathematicians. Our goal as teachers is to support and guide students as they develop both their content knowledge and their process skills, so they are able to continue to expand and refine their understanding of mathematics. This series is a guide for math educators who aspire to teach students more than math content. It is a guide to assist teachers in understanding and teaching the critical processes through which students learn and make sense of mathematics.

Susan O'Connell
Series Editor

Spending time with students and hearing their insights about mathematics has been a wonderful part of this project. We would like to thank the students who contributed work samples or allowed their photographs to be included in this book: Aanchal Agarwal, Austin Bodolay, Jakobi Bradford, Robert Carter, Gloria Cherone, Michael Croskey, Sarah Demetry, Jayna Desai, Hannah Donahoe, Nina Graziano, James Hegarty, Alex Johnson, Jennifer Le, Beth Leidich, Rachel Livengood, Tevin McDonald, Megan Morley, Shriya Murthy, Joe Neuzil, Kevin Neuzil, Joshua Omadé, Christian Portillo, Austin Price, Rachel Reindorf, and Terry Tan. It was a pleasure working with them and hearing their math conversations. Thanks to Ms. Kathleen Brady, principal of Samuel Ogle Middle School in Bowie, MD, for allowing us to work with the outstanding students at the school. Special thanks also to Beverly Fogg and Celeste McGill, teachers in Bridgeport, WV, and Bowie, MD, for sharing their students' work.

We are extremely grateful to Emily Birch, our Heinemann editor, for her guidance throughout this project. And thanks to Elizabeth Valway, our production editor, for her valuable input on all aspects of the production of this book.

To our families, who have provided us with ongoing support, we express our sincere gratitude and love. Heartfelt thanks from Sue to her family—Pat, Brendan, Katie, Jason, and Allison. Sincere gratitude from Suzanne to her husband Darrell and son Michael.

Problem-Solving Standard

Instructional programs from prekindergarten through grade 12 should enable all students to—

- build new mathematical knowledge through problem solving;

- solve problems that arise in mathematics and in other contexts;

- apply and adapt a variety of appropriate strategies to solve problems;

- monitor and reflect on the process of mathematical problem solving.

Reasoning and Proof Standard

Instructional programs from prekindergarten through grade 12 should enable all students to—

- recognize reasoning and proof as fundamental aspects of mathematics;

- make and investigate mathematical conjectures;

- develop and evaluate mathematical arguments and proofs;

- select and use various types of reasoning and methods of proof.

---

[1] Standards are listed with the permission of the National Council of Teachers of Mathematics (NCTM). NCTM does not endorse the content or validity of these alignments.

Communication Standard

Instructional programs from prekindergarten through grade 12 should enable all students to—

- organize and consolidate their mathematical thinking through communication;

- communicate their mathematical thinking coherently and clearly to peers, teachers, and others;

- analyze and evaluate the mathematical thinking and strategies of others;

- use the language of mathematics to express mathematical ideas precisely.

Connections Standard

Instructional programs from prekindergarten through grade 12 should enable all students to—

- recognize and use connections among mathematical ideas;

- understand how mathematical ideas interconnect and build on one another to produce a coherent whole;

- recognize and apply mathematics in contexts outside of mathematics.

Representation Standard

Instructional programs from prekindergarten through grade 12 should enable all students to—

- create and use representations to organize, record, and communicate mathematical ideas;

- select, apply, and translate among mathematical representations to solve problems;

- use representations to model and interpret physical, social, and mathematical phenomena.

NCTM Content Standards and Expectations for Grades 6–8

NCTM Process Standards and Expectations

NUMBER AND OPERATIONS

	Expectations
Instructional programs from prekindergarten through grade 12 should enable all students to—	**In grades 6–8 all students should—**
Understand numbers, ways of representing numbers, relationships among numbers, and number systems	• work flexibly with fractions, decimals, and percents to solve problems; • compare and order fractions, decimals, and percents efficiently and find their approximate locations on a number line; • develop meaning for percents greater than 100 and less than 1; • understand and use ratios and proportions to represent quantitative relationships; • develop an understanding of large numbers and recognize and appropriately use exponential, scientific, and calculator notation; • use factors, multiples, prime factorization, and relatively prime numbers to solve problems; • develop meaning for integers and represent and compare quantities with them.
Understand meanings of operations and how they relate to one another	• understand the meaning and effects of arithmetic operations with fractions, decimals, and integers; • use the associative and commutative properties of addition and multiplication and the distributive property of multiplication over addition to simplify computations with integers, fractions, and decimals; • understand and use the inverse relationships of addition and subtraction, multiplication and division, and squaring and finding square roots to simplify computations and solve problems

	Expectations
Instructional programs from prekindergarten through grade 12 should enable all students to—	**In grades 6–8 all students should—**
Compute fluently and make reasonable estimates	• select appropriate methods and tools for computing with fractions and decimals from among mental computation, estimation, calculators or computers, and paper and pencil, depending on the situation, and apply the selected methods; • develop and analyze algorithms for computing with fractions, decimals, and integers and develop fluency in their use; • develop and use strategies to estimate the results of rational-number computations and judge the reasonableness of the results; • develop, analyze, and explain methods for solving problems involving proportions, such as scaling and finding equivalent ratios.

ALGEBRA

	Expectations
Instructional programs from prekindergarten through grade 12 should enable all students to—	**In grades 6–8 all students should—**
Understand patterns, relations, and functions	• represent, analyze, and generalize a variety of patterns with tables, graphs, words, and, when possible, symbolic rules; • relate and compare different forms of representation for a relationship; • identify functions as linear or nonlinear and contrast their properties from tables, graphs, or equations.
Represent and analyze mathematical situations and structures using algebraic symbols	• develop an initial conceptual understanding of different uses of variables;

	Expectations
Instructional programs from prekindergarten through grade 12 should enable all students to—	**In grades 6–8 all students should—**
	• explore relationships between symbolic expressions and graphs of lines, paying particular attention to the meaning of intercept and slope;
	• use symbolic algebra to represent situations and to solve problems, especially those that involve linear relationships;
	• recognize and generate equivalent forms for simple algebraic expressions and solve linear equations
Use mathematical models to represent and understand quantitative relationships	• model and solve contextualized problems using various representations, such as graphs, tables, and equations.
Analyze change in various contexts	• use graphs to analyze the nature of changes in quantities in linear relationships.

GEOMETRY

	Expectations
Instructional programs from prekindergarten through grade 12 should enable all students to—	**In grades 6–8 all students should—**
Analyze characteristics and properties of two- and three-dimensional geometric shapes and develop mathematical arguments about geometric relationships	• precisely describe, classify, and understand relationships among types of two- and three-dimensional objects using their defining properties;
	• understand relationships among the angles, side lengths, perimeters, areas, and volumes of similar objects;
	• create and critique inductive and deductive arguments concerning geometric ideas and relationships, such as congruence, similarity, and the Pythagorean relationship.

	Expectations
Instructional programs from prekindergarten through grade 12 should enable all students to—	**In grades 6–8 all students should—**
Specify locations and describe spatial relationships using coordinate geometry and other representational systems	• use coordinate geometry to represent and examine the properties of geometric shapes;
	• use coordinate geometry to examine special geometric shapes, such as regular polygons or those with pairs of parallel or perpendicular sides.
Apply transformations and use symmetry to analyze mathematical situations	• describe sizes, positions, and orientations of shapes under informal transformations such as flips, turns, slides, and scaling;
	• examine the congruence, similarity, and line or rotational symmetry of objects using transformations.
Use visualization, spatial reasoning, and geometric modeling to solve problems	• draw geometric objects with specified properties, such as side lengths or angle measures;
	• use two-dimensional representations of three-dimensional objects to visualize and solve problems such as those involving surface area and volume;
	• use visual tools such as networks to represent and solve problems;
	• use geometric models to represent and explain numerical and algebraic relationships;
	• recognize and apply geometric ideas and relationships in areas outside the mathematics classroom, such as art, science, and everyday life.

	Expectations
Instructional programs from prekindergarten through grade 12 should enable all students to—	**In grades 6–8 all students should—**
Understand measurable attributes of objects and the units, systems, and processes of measurement	• understand both metric and customary systems of measurement; • understand relationships among units and convert from one unit to another within the same system; • understand, select, and use units of appropriate size and type to measure angles, perimeter, area, surface area, and volume.
Apply appropriate techniques, tools, and formulas to determine measurements	• use common benchmarks to select appropriate methods for estimating measurements; • select and apply techniques and tools to accurately find length, area, volume, and angle measures to appropriate levels of precision; • develop and use formulas to determine the circumference of circles and the area of triangles, parallelograms, trapezoids, and circles and develop strategies to find the area of more-complex shapes; • develop strategies to determine the surface area and volume of selected prisms, pyramids, and cylinders; • solve problems involving scale factors, using ratio and proportion; • solve simple problems involving rates and derived measurements for such attributes as velocity and density.

DATA ANALYSIS AND PROBABILITY

	Expectations
Instructional programs from prekindergarten through grade 12 should enable all students to—	**In grades 6–8 all students should—**
Formulate questions that can be addressed with data and collect, organize, and display relevant data to answer them	• formulate questions, design studies, and collect data about a characteristic shared by two populations or different characteristics within one population; • select, create, and use appropriate graphical representations of data, including histograms, box plots, and scatterplots.
Select and use appropriate statistical methods to analyze data	• find, use, and interpret measures of center and spread, including mean and interquartile range; • discuss and understand the correspondence between data sets and their graphical representations, especially histograms, stem-and-leaf plots, box plots, and scatterplots.
Develop and evaluate inferences and predictions that are based on data	• use observations about differences between two or more samples to make conjectures about the populations from which the samples were taken; • make conjectures about possible relationships between two characteristics of a sample on the basis of scatterplots of the data and approximate lines of fit; • use conjectures to formulate new questions and plan new studies to answer them.
Understand and apply basic concepts of probability	• understand and use appropriate terminology to describe complementary and mutually exclusive events; • use proportionality and a basic understanding of probability to make and test conjectures about the results of experiments and simulations; • compute probabilities for simple compound events, using such methods as organized lists, tree diagrams, and area models.

The Communication Standard

Students who have opportunities, encouragement, and support for speaking, writing, reading, and listening in mathematics classes reap dual benefits: they communicate to learn mathematics, and they learn to communicate mathematically.

—National Council of Teachers of Mathematics,
Principles and Standards for School Mathematics

Why Communicate About Mathematics?

In mathematics, as in other subject areas, talking and writing are critical processes through which students develop content understanding. Through communication, students are able to test their thinking, clarify misconceptions, discover alternate ideas, and extend their understandings. As students struggle to get their thoughts into words, they are challenged to process the ideas in order to restate them, elaborate on them, or conjecture about them. As they listen to their own and others' thinking, they often recognize their confusions, question their understandings, and fold others' ideas into their own in order to modify and refine their knowledge. As students read, write, talk, and listen, they are challenged to think, analyze, summarize, prioritize, and reflect.

Talking and writing about math allows students to monitor and assess their own thinking. In addition, it plays a critical role in the classroom assessment process. Communication, whether oral or written, allows us to know what our students are thinking. It provides us with more information than simply whether an answer is right or wrong; rather, it allows us to assess the degree to which our students understand a math skill or concept. Communication provides us with a window through which we can see their thoughts. Whether our goal is to support concept development or to provide a means of assessment, communicating about mathematical ideas plays a vital role in our mathematics classrooms.

While we recognize that communicating about content is valuable for both learning and assessing that content, communicating about math offers special challenges for many students. In mathematics, the communication process is complicated by a specialized vocabulary, an uncertainty about how to verbalize one's thinking, and the sheer complexity of some mathematical concepts. Students must be supported as they learn to communicate mathematically. We can assist our students in developing their abilities to communicate effectively about mathematics through attention to foundational skills such as vocabulary development, organization of thinking, and understanding of question/answer relationships. Teacher questioning techniques to spark student thinking and teacher modeling to illustrate ways to express mathematical ideas have tremendous benefits. Providing our students with opportunities to talk about math through cooperative learning activities and to write about math through a variety of classroom writing assignments assists students in developing their communication skills. And frequent and specific feedback helps students refine and enhance their communication skills. As we explore best practices in communicating about mathematics, we must focus on helping our students use communication as a tool to learn mathematics, while also helping them learn to communicate effectively about mathematics.

What Is the Communication Standard?

The National Council of Teachers of Mathematics (NCTM) has developed standards in order to support and guide us as we develop classroom lessons and create activities to build our students' mathematical understandings. The first five standards delineate the content to be addressed in the math classroom (Number and Operations, Algebra, Geometry, Measurement, and Data Analysis and Probability), while the next five standards address the processes through which students explore and use mathematics (Problem Solving, Reasoning and Proof, Communication, Connections, and Representation). Communication is a critical math process, and the components of the NCTM Communication Standard reflect its integral role in student learning.

Instructional programs should enable students to:

- organize and consolidate their mathematical thinking through communication

- communicate their mathematical thinking coherently and clearly to peers, teachers, and others

- analyze and evaluate the mathematical thinking and strategies of others

- use the language of mathematics to express mathematical ideas precisely (NCTM 2000, 60)

Throughout this book, we explore ways to assist students in developing and refining their thinking through verbal and written communication. We investigate communication activities that build students' math understanding and delve into a variety of ways to strengthen students' communication skills so they are better able to talk and write about math content. We identify techniques for strengthening their familiarity with and use of the complex language of math so they are better able to put their math thinking into words. And we explore ways to get students to listen to the thoughts of others and reflect on each other's ideas and strategies. The NCTM Communication Standard guides our transition from silent math classrooms filled with rows of students completing paper-and-pencil drills to classrooms in which individuals, pairs, or groups of students are actively engaged in talking, writing, and reflecting about math ideas.

How This Book Will Help You

This book is designed to help you better understand the NCTM process standard of communication. It explores communication as a process through which students learn mathematics and as a skill that enables students to express the mathematics they have learned. This book focuses specifically on the mathematical goals of students in the middle grades (grades 6 through 8) and offers practical ideas for helping them communicate effectively about mathematics.

This book addresses a variety of significant topics related to the communication standard. The importance of teacher talk to express and model ideas is explored, as well as ideas for teacher questioning techniques to promote student reflection and discussion. A variety of classroom activities that promote discourse through partner, small-group, and whole-class discussions are included, as are strategies to aid students in increasing their math vocabularies and strengthening their skills in reading math text. Attention is given to the challenges of writing about math, and specific strategies are offered to support students as they learn to effectively record their math understandings. Suggestions for improving the quality of students' writing through varied feedback techniques are included, as well as tips for selecting meaningful writing tasks and scoring students' writing assignments.

Once we have explored the communication standard in depth, we examine the standard as it connects to math content in Chapter 9, titled "Communication Across the Content Standards". Through sample classroom activities, we explore the interconnectedness of the content and process standards. You will see student work to illustrate these lessons and will be asked to reflect on the teaching of math content through communication, as well as the teaching of communication skills in the context of mathematics.

Examples of student work are presented throughout the book to offer a glimpse into students' mathematical thinking and communication, and classroom-tested tips are shared to provide you with practical ideas to better meet the needs of your students. Following each chapter, several questions for discussion prompt you to think about the content presented in the chapter, whether alone or with a group of your colleagues. The accompanying CD is filled with a variety of teacher-ready materials to make it easier for you to implement the ideas explored throughout the chapters. Graphic organizers, rubrics, and a parent letter are all included on the CD, along with a wealth of math writing activities that connect specifically to the math content for grades 6 through 8. All of the CD resources are customizable, allowing you to modify them (i.e., alter the problem situation, change the data, or insert your students' names), providing you with a practical tool for meeting the needs of varied levels of students within your classroom.

This book was written to provide you with both theory and practical resources for building your students' math communication skills. It is hoped that this book enhances your understanding of the communication standard and provides you with insights and practical ideas to further develop your students' skills. As we better understand the importance of verbal and written communication in our math classrooms and the challenges facing students as they attempt to talk and write about their math thinking, we are better able to identify, select, and design meaningful tasks.

It is hoped that the varied instructional practices highlighted in this book assist you in developing your students' skills as well as expanding your own understanding of the communication standard. The more we reflect on the role of communication in our math classrooms, the more we are able to recognize its benefits to our students in both helping them learn mathematics and in helping them effectively express the math they have learned.

Questions for Discussion

1. Do you remember talking and writing in your math classrooms when you were a student? Was communicating about your thinking encouraged and valued?

2. Why might we want to do away with quiet math classrooms? How might talk about mathematics support our students' understanding of math?

3. In what ways is writing used as a tool for learning content? Think about times when students are asked to write in other subject areas. What are some benefits of asking students to write about their thinking?

CHAPTER 1

Exploring the Role of Communication in Middle Grades Mathematics

Like a piece of music, the classroom discourse has themes that pull together to create a whole that has meaning. The teacher has a central role in orchestrating the oral and written discourse in ways that contribute to students' understanding of mathematics.

—National Council of Teachers of Mathematics, *Professional Standards for Teaching Mathematics*

It is likely that communication did not play a major role in math classrooms when you were a student. Many people recall silent math classrooms in which they did math computations, but rarely discussed methods, strategies, or solutions. Writing consisted of numbers or representations, perhaps diagrams or graphs, but rarely involved the writing of ideas in words. Math classrooms that revolve around the communication skills of listening, speaking, reading, and writing may not feel familiar to many of us, but throughout this chapter we explore critical reasons why classrooms that focus on communication help bring math understanding to our students and afford considerable benefits to both students and teachers.

We are quick to recognize the challenges when classroom discussions and open-ended writing are introduced into our math lessons. We know that it takes longer to say or write a justification than it does to state or record an answer. We acknowledge that it is difficult for many students to express their math understanding in words, and we concede that scoring writing tasks is more complex and more time-consuming than simply scoring for correct answers. Without a strong belief that communication will both enhance our teaching and enhance our students' learning, the challenges seem to outweigh the benefits. But as we further explore communication in mathematics, a greater insight into its value in the teaching and learning of mathematics can help us better deal with the classroom challenges it might present.

Weighing the Benefits of Communicating About Math

We use receptive communication skills, listening and reading, to gather and acquire information. We use expressive communication skills—talking and writing—to express information to others. But communication also requires us to process the ideas in order to understand them and to organize the ideas in order to express them. Through communication, we gather, refine, and express our understandings. So how can communication processes be best used in middle grades classrooms? How can these processes extend students' understanding of mathematics? How can they support teachers who work to build students' math knowledge and skills?

Benefits for Students

Communication is active. Rather than simply listening to a lecture, students discuss, debate, display, predict, organize, conjecture, record, generalize, and justify their ideas. They are actively involved in the learning process. Ideas become group property, with everyone building upon each other's thoughts. Through communication, students hear others' ideas, blend those ideas with their own, and continue to refine their thinking (see Figure 1–1).

Many people process ideas as they talk or write about those ideas. Have you ever read out loud when studying for a test? Did hearing the words help you process and remember the ideas? Have you written notes when studying from a book? Although

Figure 1–1 *Collaborating to explore math ideas engages and motivates students.*

you are rewriting what is written on the pages of the book, did writing the ideas help you better focus on them, absorb them, or retain them?

Opportunities for discussions, or for repeated or alternate explanations, bolster our understanding of ideas. When you were still confused after a math lesson, did you ever go home and sit at the kitchen table with your father or mother or older sibling and ask them to talk you through the math lesson? Did you need to hear it one more time or in a different way? Did you need to ask questions to clarify the ideas? Would you like to build those discussions into your lessons so you are there to guide students, restate ideas, and answer their questions?

Communication helps students recognize what they know and what they don't know. Have you ever thought you understood an idea or a procedure, nodding in agreement as someone explained the ideas, but when asked to restate the ideas, quickly recognized that your understanding was not solid? As we talk, we hear our own thoughts and are often able to identify our own misunderstandings. Many students develop clearer understandings after verbalizing their ideas and listening to their own words. For example, Elizabeth tried to explain how to change a decimal to a percent, but partway through her explanation said, "Wait—that can't be right. I'm not sure." Her partner talked her through the process one more time. Elizabeth commented, "Oh, yeah, now I get it." (Maybe Elizabeth should try restating it again, just to be sure!)

The ability to clearly communicate ideas is a goal for our students in all content areas. Communication in math class provides an opportunity for students to practice and apply the reading, writing, listening, and speaking skills they learn during their language arts lessons. Reading the math textbook provides a real example of content text and challenges students to test and apply reading strategies. Writing about math provides opportunities to apply writing skills to difficult content. The goals of reading and language arts classes are for students to be able to apply their skills to real situations, like the learning of mathematics.

Group and partner work, writing activities, and class discussions are all vital ways to motivate and engage students in the middle grades. Rather than consisting of silent rows of students doing computation after computation, our classrooms become lively forums for discussions, group projects, and partner tasks. Even those students who were successful in the old drill-and-practice approach often report that math class was "boring." Few students looked forward to doing long sets of silent computations.

Along with motivating students by providing more engaging lessons, communication can reduce students' anxiety. Communication can become a way for students to express their feelings of competence or insecurity, perhaps through journal writing. Communication can provide an opportunity to receive emotional or academic support from peers, through group or partner work. It can help students see others' frustrations and know that they are not alone in their confusions or provide them with partner support as they struggle to understand a concept or procedure. It can bolster their confidence as they work with groups to explore ideas or solve problems.

Benefits for Teachers

While there are many reasons why incorporating communication into our math lessons will benefit students, there are also many ways in which it informs and enhances our teaching. Whether students are telling us their ideas, sharing their ideas with a partner, or writing about their understandings, communication gives us a unique opportunity to assess what students are thinking. We are able to see what they have learned and to identify their misunderstandings or partial understandings. As an assessment tool, communication allows us to see more than simply a right or wrong answer. It allows us to probe into a deeper level of students' understanding. Did they get the right answer? Can they explain how they did it and why it made sense to do it that way? Talk and writing allow us to move our students beyond basic skills to assess if they are able to understand and apply those skills.

Talk and writing in the math classroom allow us to monitor students' perceptions of the difficulty of the task (e.g., Did they find it to be easy? Hard?) and allow us to monitor their confusion or frustration with the content being taught. Our knowledge of our students' feelings and frustrations helps us to maintain a classroom environment that is positive, supportive, productive, and non-threatening. Staying aware of students' feelings allows us to provide encouragement and support when needed, and to identify when modifying lessons might be important for students' skill development and morale.

One very significant benefit of incorporating talk and writing into math lessons is its value in teacher self-reflection. Through our students' comments, whether oral or written, we see what they know and do not know. Rather than using that knowledge simply to assess our students, many of us have found it invaluable as a self-reflection tool—a way to reflect on our own practices to gain insight into what we do to effectively help students understand mathematics. Did assigning the activity as a partner task support some of our struggling learners? Did we ask them to write too quickly before they had organized and processed their ideas? Are more class discussions needed to strengthen understanding of this concept? Analyzing student talk and writing as it relates to our own teaching practices can lead us to refine our skills and help us identify the instructional strategies that are making a difference for our students.

By incorporating communication tasks into our math lessons, we are able to effectively address both content and process standards. While exploring key math content, communication activities allow us to pose group problem-solving tasks, stimulate reasoning through whole-class discussions, encourage the representation of ideas through written assignments, or make connections between math concepts through oral or written discussions. Communication elevates math to a thinking skill rather than a rote skill. It allows us to move beyond just doing math and push students to understand, to explore, and to explain math ideas.

CLASSROOM-TESTED TIP

Why Write in Math Class?

Students often ask: "Why do I have to write in math class?" Let's be honest, we wondered the same thing when writing began to appear in math classrooms! Have discussions with your students to share why writing is important in all content areas. Link writing in math to writing about a piece of literature in

English, writing about an investigation in science, or writing about a historic event in social studies. Remind students that writing helps us sort out our ideas, figure out what we know or don't know, and gather insights or draw conclusions. Remind them that writing is a way we share our ideas, and reading what they have written will help you to know their ideas. Tell them that you will support them if it gets hard to write about tough math ideas and that you will share tips to help them get their ideas out of their heads and onto the paper (see the many tips in Chapters 5 and 6). Acknowledge that writing in math may get difficult at times, but that you will be there to support them!

Creating an Environment in Which Communication Flourishes

Is math simply content to be presented and memorized, or is it content to be processed, discussed, explored, and ultimately, understood? Is math about a correct answer, or is it about juggling ideas and figuring out concepts so that we are able to generalize about ideas, connect concepts, and find solutions? If students are to be asked to explore the content of math, an often complex and confusing content, then it is critical that we create classroom environments in which students are comfortable expressing their ideas. They must feel comfortable sharing solid reasoning and accurate answers as well as expressing illogical conjectures, making inaccurate predictions, and suggesting unreasonable procedures. The success of communication as a tool for understanding math depends on students' willingness to communicate openly. So what type of environment will promote student discussions? What can we do to help students feel comfortable sharing their ideas, even if they are not sure of the correctness of those ideas?

Creating a nonthreatening atmosphere is an important factor in getting students to talk about their mathematical thinking. Nothing will stifle communication more quickly than getting negative reactions from teachers or other students. If students believe that a right answer is the goal of answering questions, they may not volunteer an answer out of fear of being wrong. Many teachers have found it helpful to transition from traditional evaluative comments (e.g., "good," "right," or "great idea") to responses that clarify the student's comments or prompt for further ideas (i.e., "So you are saying . . . Does anyone want to add to that?"). It may feel awkward at first, but it will begin to refocus students on listening to each other's ideas rather than on seeking your approval. The goal of student communication is to extend and refine students' understanding of math ideas, which means that illogical comments or incorrect responses are part of the process. Teachers who use student comments, whether right or wrong, to build greater understanding of the math ideas are making the most of the communication process.

Students in the middle grades benefit from talking about classroom expectations. Class discussions, during which teachers share their expectations for student involvement in discussions, help relieve students' anxiety. Miss Price, an eighth-grade teacher, stresses that everyone's ideas are valued and that no ideas should be laughed at or dismissed. She begins the year by asking her students to work in teams to develop a list of expectations for class discussions and then has teams report their ideas and work together to select class expectations that are posted on her classroom wall. Some of her students' suggestions are listed below:

> Listen to everyone's ideas.
> We should all share our ideas.
> Let everyone finish what they are saying.
> Don't laugh at any ideas.
> It's okay to be wrong.

Equity is a major factor in developing a positive environment. Rather than calling on students whose hands are raised or who are seated at the front of the room, making an effort to call on all students sets the tone for a classroom in which all students are respected and all comments are valued.

While we want all of our students to be involved in class discussions, we recognize that students process questions and formulate their answers at varied speeds. Simple strategies like think-pair-share (Kagan 1992) in which students first think silently about the question, then are prompted to turn to a partner to talk about their answer, and finally are asked to raise their hands to share their answer with the whole class, provide students with time to process their ideas and an opportunity to test their ideas on a partner before volunteering to share them with the class. This simple technique, which takes just a couple of minutes, relieves students' insecurity and maximizes their involvement in class discussions, and it can be particularly valuable for ELL (English language learners) or struggling students as it ensures both wait time and partner discussions. And for middle grades students, who can be extremely sensitive to their classmates' reactions, the ability to discuss and refine their ideas with a partner prior to announcing them to the class can alleviate anxiety and boost confidence.

Supporting students who struggle with talking about mathematics is critical if we want to develop a climate in which all students feel comfortable talking. It may be that your struggling or reluctant learners could be lured into class discussions with less-threatening contributions in which they might restate others' ideas or be asked simpler questions until they feel more comfortable expressing their ideas. And we must keep in mind that some students may have less to say than others and may benefit greatly from listening to classroom conversations. A reluctance to share ideas may indicate a student's confusion about the math concept. Further listening to others' comments may help clarify those ideas. Or finding a time to chat privately (i.e., while others are involved in a class assignment or group task) may provide an opportunity to check their understanding and offer subtle support. Our sensitivity, combined with our intuition to know when to ask students to speak and when to allow them to listen, helps shy or reluctant students build their confidence. Our goal is to involve all students in communicating their ideas, but the pace at which they become comfortable sharing those ideas may differ greatly among students.

Creating a Community of Learners

Developing a positive classroom environment includes building a feeling of community. Students need to know that they are learning together. At times, they will share their confusion. At other times, they will celebrate their insights. Developing this community of learners is essential for a classroom to have positive, productive, and interactive communication.

Traditionally, the teacher asked the question and the student answered it. The teacher then commented on the correctness of the response and moved on to the next question. All of the communication was teacher-to-student or student-to-teacher. An essential dynamic for a classroom that is focused on communication is student-to-student discourse. In the middle grades, students should be encouraged to interact with each other and build on each other's ideas. As teachers develop and discuss their expectations, student-to-student discourse should be a part of those discussions. Teachers must make it clear that students should be listening to others' ideas, and that building on others' ideas is not only acceptable but highly encouraged. Teachers may need to praise students who mention others' ideas in their comments (e.g., "I liked the way you used Jon's idea to get started and then added your own thoughts to it.") as an ongoing reminder of this expectation. If students are not listening to others, many teachers have found that asking students to paraphrase their classmates' ideas can help focus their attention on listening (e.g., "Who can say that in another way?" or "Who can restate what Heather just said?").

Language-Rich Classrooms

Paying attention to the physical arrangement of the classroom can aid in creating an optimal environment for math communication. In classrooms where students are frequently asked to work in groups or share ideas with partners, teachers often opt to arrange desks in groups rather than in the more traditional rows. Having students' desks already positioned near a partner allows for quick sharing opportunities without the need for rearranging furniture.

Classrooms that promote communication are language rich. Bulletin boards displaying student work contribute to the positive environment by acknowledging the value of students' ideas. Bulletin boards can be used as teaching tools, displaying a problem of the week, writing prompt, or critical-thinking question, or they can be interactive forums on which students might use posted clues to guess vocabulary words or complete math challenges. Using bulletin boards in these ways illustrates your ongoing expectation for communication and reasoning about the math ideas. Word walls, displaying critical math vocabulary, support students by allowing them to reference the words if they struggle to express their math ideas during class discussions. Blackboards, whiteboards, overhead projectors, chart paper, or video visualizers (document viewers) provide opportunities for teachers to write as they talk, supporting those students who benefit from seeing and hearing the words and allowing students to show their work as they talk about their thinking (see Figure 1–2). The availability of manipulatives provides a way for students to show their ideas when the words are difficult to find. And classroom centers may provide non-threatening places for students to communicate with partners or groups to complete collaborative math projects.

Creating an environment that promotes communication is about modifying our expectations from quiet students to verbal students and from correct answers to reflective thinking. It is about developing a community of learners who respect each other's ideas, whether right or wrong, and who work to support each other in building math understanding.

CLASSROOM-TESTED TIP

Encouraging Communication

It is easy to lapse into calling on students who raise their hands quickly, but developing a climate that promotes good discussions requires that all students have a chance to share their ideas. Try the following ideas to get more students involved in class discussions.

Wait a Minute

After asking a question, ask students to keep their hands down for a minute. Have a signal (e.g., raise your own hand) to indicate when they may raise their hands. The extra time is important to students who take a bit longer to process the ideas, and you will notice a greater number of students raising their hands to respond to your question.

Turn and Share

After asking a question, routinely give students a quick chance to share with a partner to ensure that they have thought about the ideas and had a chance to test them out on someone else. This takes just a minute and relieves anxiety for students who might be insecure about their answers. After talking with a partner, students often feel more confident and are ready to share their ideas with others.

Get Them Started

If you have posed a question that has multiple answers, get students jumpstarted by providing one answer to help them understand what you are asking. Perhaps you asked students to give you examples of times when you might need to understand percentages or situations in which you would need to find a perimeter. Consider calling on your struggling students early in the process, before too many answers have been given, and calling on your more able students a little later to challenge them to find examples beyond the most obvious ones.

Figure 1–2 *This student explains his math thinking to
his classmates who are able to see his work with the
aid of a video visualizer.*

Communication as Raising the Bar

So, why add communication to our middle school math classrooms? Writing a number answer is one level of math knowledge. Adding the process of communication is raising the bar to a higher level. We are no longer satisfied with a simple number answer; we want to ensure that our students understand how they got that answer, can justify the process they used, or can generalize whether that process always works. We know that mathematics will get much more sophisticated as students enter high school, and we want to ensure that they have a strong foundation on which to continue to build their math skills.

Through communication tasks, we push our students to know math in a deeper way. We ask them to tell us why, how, and what if. Through communication, we connect the math process and content standards, providing students with a way to process and express their understanding about varied math content. Communicating about math is not easy for many students because it asks difficult questions. It asks for more than a memorization of facts. It requires students to hear ideas, process those ideas, make them their own, and then express their understandings. Throughout the remaining chapters of this book, we explore a variety of ways to make the most of communication within your classroom. We discuss strategies and activities that use communication to support your students' content understanding. We explore ideas for strengthening the skills of those students who struggle to communicate about math, and we discuss the critical role of communication in accurately assessing students' understanding and guiding our instructional planning.

Questions for Discussion

1. How does communicating about mathematics benefit students? How does hearing or seeing students' communications about mathematics benefit teachers?

2. How might listening to students' comments, either oral or written, help us refine our teaching methods? After reviewing a set of student work samples for student assessment purposes, review them again to reflect on your teaching methods. What did you do within your lesson that contributed to the success of the students? Do you think students might have done better if you had set up the task in a different way? Did they need more time to discuss ideas? What can you do differently next time that might improve their work?

3. What might you see and hear in a math classroom that values communication?

4. In what ways might a teacher help reluctant students feel comfortable and willing to share their ideas?

5. How might a teacher promote communication through the physical arrangement of the classroom? Analyze your classroom arrangement. Can adjustments be made to better promote communication?

CHAPTER 2

Providing a Context for Math Talk

Students need to work with mathematical tasks that are worthwhile topics of discussion.

—National Council of Teachers of Mathematics,
Principles and Standards for School Mathematics

We have noted that there are many benefits when students communicate about mathematics, but engaging middle grades students in productive discussions about their math ideas can be a challenge. How do we get our students talking about math? What can we do to provide a context through which our students can talk about math ideas that are often abstract and difficult to express? We must find ways to stimulate discussions about important math ideas and provide a context through which students can begin to share their understandings. Problem tasks, manipulative activities, and links to literature or real-world experiences provide a jumping-off point for math talk. And the types of questions and prompts that are posed to students serve to stimulate productive discussions and lead to meaningful writing assignments. In this chapter, we explore a variety of ways to get students talking about math.

The Role of Questioning

One of the benefits of talk in the math classroom is that it helps build students' understanding of math ideas. That does not happen in classrooms where students are asked for only the answer. Students must be asked questions that get them talking about important concepts, ask them to elaborate on their thinking, push them to listen to others, ask them to summarize important ideas, and encourage them to delve deeper into math procedures and solutions.

Think back on your own experiences as a student in a math classroom. Do you remember correcting your homework or quiz with a different-colored marker or switching papers with the student sitting next to you? As correct answers were rattled off, did you place an X by any that were incorrect on the paper in front of you? Did hearing the right answer help you understand why your answer was wrong? Would it have been helpful to hear how to get the right answer? The questioning that took place in many math classrooms did not help us expand our understanding by probing into why an answer was correct or clarifying how to do the procedure. Rather, in many cases, it frustrated those who did not get the right answer and provided little or no insight to support them in the future. Would you have benefited from discussions about such questions as "How did you get that answer?" "Did anyone get the answer in a different way?" or "What was confusing about that problem?" Those questions might have sparked insights about important math ideas and procedures and might have helped you recognize errors in your thinking or clarified procedures that you did not fully understand.

Questioning is a powerful instructional tool. Through our selection of just the right question we can accomplish many goals. Certainly, there are many questions that can be answered with simply a number or a *yes* or *no* response. While there is nothing wrong with asking such questions, students' responses provide only a glimpse of their understanding at a basic level. Our goal is to probe into students' thinking and learn more about the decisions they make, the procedures they use, and the reasoning that supports their actions. Our questioning can prompt a recall of facts or it can stimulate deeper thought about math ideas. Our awareness of the types of questions we ask is vital. The more we recognize and analyze our own questioning behaviors, the more we can effectively use questioning to enhance communication and strengthen math understanding within our classrooms.

A very basic goal of questioning is to ask students to state information or recall ideas—for example:

"What are ratios?"
"Define independent events."
"What are the characteristics of a triangular pyramid?"

When we ask students these questions, we are probing for their knowledge about the ideas or concepts. While these questions ask for recall of ideas, they are posed in an open way so that students must share more of their understanding than if we had asked a closed question (e.g., "What do we call two lines that are the same distance apart at all points and never cross?"). Closed questions are simply answered with a word or phrase (e.g., "parallel lines"), a number, or a *yes* or *no* response. Asking recall questions in an open format stimulates deeper student thinking.

Often student responses are brief or unclear and our questions continue to push their thinking or help them, or others, to clarify the ideas:

"So a cylinder is a solid figure. What else can you tell me about a cylinder?"
"So you see a functional relationship between these numbers. Can you tell me how they are related?"

In addition to probing for more detail, these questions also promote collaboration and discussion. Student responses are respected, and students are encouraged to listen to each other's comments and respond to and expand on them:

"Will Peter's idea work?"
"Do you agree with Ming?"

Asking students to restate others' ideas, or ideas from a lesson or text, offers insights into their personal understanding:

"Can you restate that idea in your own words?"
"Are you saying that 25% is less than 1/3? Can you explain that?"

These questions push students to express their thoughts and possibly rethink their ideas as they talk them through. The process of restating ideas often helps students clarify their thinking.

Questions that ask students to expand on their ideas and justify their answers push them to think more deeply about the mathematics they are discussing. Rather than simply asking for the answer, asking students *how* and *why* questions requires them to fully understand and defend their responses. After students have solved a problem, we might ask them some *how* questions:

"How did you solve the problem?"
"Explain the steps you took to get to the solution."

Or we might ask students to defend their answers or their methods with some *why* questions:

"Why do you believe he is more likely to pick a red cube?"
"Why did you use a table to solve that problem?"

Listening to students' responses sheds a great deal of light on the level of their understanding. And asking students to be aware of their own thinking (metacognition) helps them to identify their own thought processes and better understand the path they took in solving a problem:

"What was hard about that problem?"
"What did you do when you got stuck?"

Another very important role of questioning is to help students make connections between concepts to better clarify their understanding:

"How are ratios and proportions alike? How are they different?"
"What are the similarities and differences between decimals and percents?"

These questions prompt students to explore and express ideas through comparisons, a very helpful way of pushing students to delve deeper into their understanding of each separate item as well as the connections between them.

Questions can also highlight connections to previous lessons:

"Where have we seen something like this before?"
"What does this problem remind you of?"

Or questions can highlight real-world connections to make the math meaningful:

"When might you want to be sure an event is fair?"
"When might you need to know how to estimate?"

Questions prompt students to think about data, to predict, to generalize, and to draw conclusions. After looking at a graph, we might ask:

"What trends do you see?"
"Why do you think the data looks that way?"

After a probability investigation, we might prompt:

"What conclusions can you draw based on the data you collected?"

Critical questions to ask in math class are questions that ask students to summarize their ideas:

"Can you tell me what you know about surface area?"
"What are some important things to remember when multiplying decimals?"

These questions ask students to sort through what they have learned, identify key ideas, and express those ideas. These questions are wonderful ways to end lessons, because they challenge students to recall, restate, and synthesize ideas discussed throughout the lesson.

Our ability to find the right question to spur discussions, stimulate thought, and promote interaction is vital. Understanding the types of questions at our disposal and selecting those that meet our needs during the course of a lesson are important skills to cultivate. Many teachers find it helpful to brainstorm key questions as they plan their lessons. Other questions will surely arise as we listen to students' comments, but recording some that are essential to our lesson objectives helps to guide our lesson. When planning lessons, consider asking questions that motivate and engage, guide the development of ideas, challenge thinking, promote reflection, and help students connect and summarize learning. Such questions will create an environment in which talk becomes an important vehicle for learning about mathematics.

Student-Generated Questions

Students need something to talk about in math class. In order to prompt rich discussions we pose thoughtful questions that stimulate higher-order thinking and communication. But don't forget the value of asking students to generate questions about math data. Display a graph, like the one in Figure 2–1, for students to analyze and discuss.

Students were asked to work with partners to design math questions for the graph data. After a few examples with the whole class, students designed questions like the following:

- How many gallons of ice cream were sold in October?

- In which month was the most ice cream sold?

- In which month was the least ice cream sold?

While their first questions were very typical, students began to look at the data more carefully, and creatively, as they continued to generate questions:

- How many gallons of ice cream were sold in the summer months (June, July, August)?

- What was the ratio of gallons sold in summer months to gallons sold in winter months (December, January, February)?

- What was the median number of gallons of ice cream sold each month for this year? What was the mean? Range?

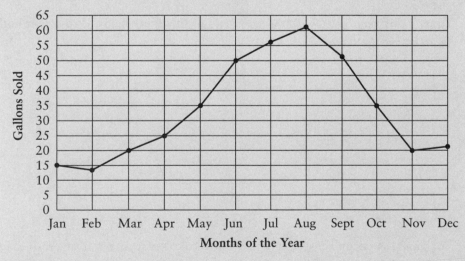

Figure 2–1 *Graphs provide intriguing data for math writing and discussions.*

■ If the owner wanted to take a two-week vacation, when would you suggest he take it? Why?

Writing their own questions pushed these students to carefully observe and analyze the graph data, and student-developed questions are perfect as a warm-up activity at the start of the next day's math lesson.

Problem Tasks to Get Them Talking

Problem-based tasks are a great way to get students talking about math. Building on our understanding of the power of our questions, we can find ways to design problem tasks that go beyond literal skills and challenge students to think more deeply and apply their skills to problem situations. Consider the following two tasks.

Task 1
What is the area of this figure?

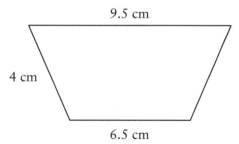

Task 2
Draw a different figure with the same area as the figure below. Prove that both figures have the same area.

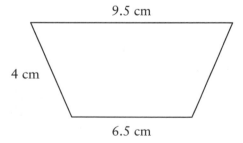

For Task 1, students must simply know how to calculate the area of a trapezoid. Memorizing the procedure would allow them to correctly answer the question. In Task 2, students must understand the concept of *area* as well as know how to calculate it. They must be able to determine the area of the given figure and then know how to create another figure with the same area. They are also asked to verbalize their understanding as they prove that the areas are the same. This task sets the stage for thinking, talking, and writing about the math ideas.

In exploring circumference, we might pose the following task:

Task 1
In art class, Jenny made a rope braid and glued it around the edge of her circular picture to create a colorful border. How much rope braiding was needed to go completely around the circular picture? Explain how you got your answer.

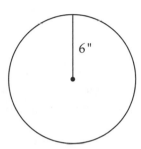

This is a good question. It requires students to think about a problem situation, decide on a way to approach the problem, and apply their knowledge about finding the circumference of a circle to find the solution. It also asks students to explain the process they used to get to their answer.

Task 2
In art class, Ms. Jones asked her students to create rope braids and then glue them around the edge of their pictures to create colorful borders. Jenny cut out the braiding she needed to border the circular picture below, but just before she glued it onto the picture she changed her mind. She decided she would rather use her rope braid to border a rectangular picture. Design a rectangle that would use about the same amount of braiding that Jenny has already cut out. Justify your answer using math data.

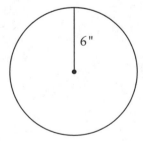

This task requires all of the thinking in Task 1, but it does not stop there. In Task 2, students must recognize the relationship between the circumference of a circle and the perimeter of a rectangle and must know how to determine the dimensions of a rectangle that would have a perimeter similar to that of the circle. Additional reasoning skills are added to the task as well as the ability to then justify the decision to prove that the rope braid will work with the rectangular picture. Not every student will create a rectangle with the same dimensions, so multiple answers are possible, but all answers must be reasonable and match the circumference of the circle. Adding complexity to problem tasks promotes deeper thinking and stimulates conversation about the tasks.

When designing problem tasks for your students, consider tasks that:

- Ask students to do more than simple calculations;

- Ask students to extend or apply their thinking;

- Ask students to explain or justify their thinking;

- May have more than one answer.

Students become engaged by problem tasks and will have lots to talk and write about as they brainstorm plans for solving them, work to execute their plans, and justify their solutions.

Using Manipulatives to Stimulate Conversations

Manipulative tasks provide students with experiences during which they must observe, analyze, and discuss math ideas (see Figure 2–2). Mrs. King gave her sixth-grade students two-color counters to explore addition of integers. As students represented each

Figure 2–2 *Hands-on activities stimulate conversations about math concepts.*

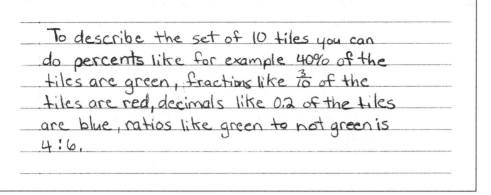

Figure 2–3 *This student describes a set of 10 color tiles, showing her
understanding of a variety of numeration concepts.*

equation with the specific amount of yellow counters (positive numbers) or red counters (negative numbers), they discussed, represented, and solved the equations. As students removed any red and yellow pairs (knowing that a red and a yellow counter
together equal zero), they were able to see the sums and had repeated opportunities to
talk about and absorb the idea of adding integers.

Mr. Newell asked his seventh-grade students to use mirrors to explore line symmetry in the letters of the alphabet. Students worked in pairs to examine the letters,
testing for line symmetry with the mirrors (looking for one half of the object to be a
mirror image of the other half). Students were then asked to sketch the letters that had
line symmetry, marking the line(s) of symmetry on their sketch, and then to define line
symmetry.

Ms. Mannix provided her eighth-graders with bags of 20 color cubes, contain-
ing some cubes that were red, blue, and yellow. Students were asked to design and
conduct a probability investigation in which they repeatedly picked a cube and replaced it in the bag Through the data collected in their hands-on investigations students were asked to predict the number of cubes of each color in their bags.

In each case, the ability to use a manipulative, as well as the problem investigation, spurred lots of communication about the math ideas. In Figure 2–3, a sixth-grade
student describes a set of color tiles demonstrating her understanding of fractions,
decimals, percents, and ratios. The manipulatives provide a context for her to talk
about her math ideas.

Talking About Children's Literature

Children's literature provides a fun and engaging way for students to hear about
and talk about math ideas. Through story events or data, students can see math in
action. While we often think of integrating children's literature into elementary math
lessons, there are many interesting books that provide a context for middle grades

math concepts. Students are able to see the application of math skills to real situations as they follow the growth of T. J. the Tiger, documented through a variety of graphs, in Ann Whitehead Nagda's book *Tiger Math* (2000). Sixth-graders were asked to discuss the reason why the author chose to use a circle graph to show the data about tigers left in the wild. They explained their ideas:

> "Because it is about all of the tigers and so the circle is all of them and the parts show how many of each kind."
>
> "It was a good idea because you can see each kind of tiger by looking at the sections and know which type of tiger has more left in the wild."
>
> "It's easy to get the idea of which kind of tiger has more when you look at the size of each section of the circle. We can see that more than half of them are Bengal tigers because that section is more than half of the circle."

Later in the lesson, the teacher asked the students to describe a *circle graph*. For many of the students, the story context aided them in explaining their ideas as they used examples from the story to illustrate their understanding.

How Much Is a Million? by David M. Schwartz (1985), explores very large numbers through fun facts shared by Marvelosissimo, the magician (e.g., To count from one to one million would take about 23 days). In a note from the author, Schwartz explains how he calculated the facts. After hearing the story and discussing the author's note, the students in Miss Robert's class were challenged to construct their own fact and justify their calculations. Kerry and Jaden determined that "If a million paper clips were clipped together they would reach from College Park to Baltimore." They explained their thinking:

> 1 paper clip = 2 inches
> 1,000,000 paper clips = 2,000,000 inches
>> "We divided 2,000,000 inches by 12 to figure out that it is about 166,666 feet. Then we knew that there are 5,280 feet in a mile so we divided 166,666 by 5,280 to find out that it is about 31.57 miles. We looked on a map and used the map scale and found that it is about 30 miles from College Park to Baltimore so we knew that our paper clips would reach about that far."

Sir Cumference and the First Round Table by Cindy Neuschwander (1997) explores the concepts of radius, diameter, and circumference through a creative story set in medieval times. After hearing the story, students might discuss the relationship between the radius and diameter of a circle and create circle study guides listing the key concepts illustrated through the story. *Anno's Mysterious Multiplying Jar* (Anno and Anno 1983) sets a context for discussions about factorials and provides a starting point for further discussions and problem-solving activities to enhance students' understanding of the concept. *The Math Curse* by Jon Scieszka and Lane Smith (1995) tells the story of a student who has a math curse and sees math problems in every situation faced throughout the day. Discussions of problem-solving strategies or engaging students in writing word problems about everyday events are natural extensions of this story.

Children's literature generates high interest and is a wonderful springboard for math discussions and investigations. Literature helps students see math situations, analyze math ideas, and express their math thinking. Through the story situations and the characters' actions, students are able to better understand math concepts and find the words and examples to explain their understanding.

Talking About Real Data

Using real data is a catalyst for math talk in the middle grades. Having students engage in problem-solving activities using data from authentic materials, such as the newspaper, travel brochures, menus, catalogs, sports playing cards, or grocery ads provides many opportunities for students to talk about math ideas. For example, students might compare and order decimals using the batting average data found on baseball cards. They might apply their understanding of percents by explaining how they determined the cost of items from a clothing store ad (e.g., 25% off the regular price of $45.00) or determined the shipping cost for a CD offer (e.g., 8% shipping on all orders). They might apply their problem-solving skills to find the best buy on necessities for Thanksgiving dinner using data from a grocery ad or find a way to feed five friends with only $35.00 using a local restaurant menu. Along with giving students the opportunity to apply classroom skills, students have opportunities to communicate about their mathematical thinking during class discussions or group tasks related to real data. As you become aware of the role that real-world materials can play in your classroom, you will discover an abundance of materials that will motivate your students and stimulate meaningful, authentic mathematics discussions.

Ensuring Productive Talk

As teachers, we face an ongoing challenge to get all of our goals accomplished during our allotted math instructional time. There are so many standards, and our students come to us at varied levels of understanding. We have procedural skills to teach and thinking skills to refine. We have math content to explore and math processes to develop. And it is understandable that we might hesitate to *discuss* ideas that we could *tell* in much less time. But we recognize the many benefits of student talk, so we need to ensure that the talk we promote within our math classrooms is productive talk. We need to keep students focused on the math.

During class discussions it is inevitable that student comments may draw the discussions in various directions. It is the teacher's role to pull the discussions back on track. We must hone our skills at keeping the focus on the math and guiding the discussion to achieve the lesson goals. At times, it might mean briefly veering off from the expected discussion and capitalizing on the insights shared by students (i.e., "How does Kenny's idea relate to what we just said?"). At other times it might be best to acknowledge comments, but table further discussions (i.e., "That's an interesting observation. We'll discuss that more later when we talk about . . ."), to ensure that the discussion achieves its purpose. During class discussions it will be important to choose which student comments you are going to elaborate on and which will be skipped over.

Finding Real Math Data

Look for real-world data to motivate and excite your students. Travel brochures, restaurant menus, sports trading cards, catalogs, and grocery store ads are all great sources for data, and the daily newspaper has a wealth of data from sports statistics to weather data to advertisements. And children's almanacs or books with intriguing data about unusual records are perfect for students in the middle grades! Can you compare the height of class members to the heights of the world's tallest or shortest people? Can you compare the speed at which athletes run to the speeds of various animals? Be creative and have fun with real data!

Here are some quick ideas for using real data:

Travel Brochures

Find a travel brochure with admission cost data. Have students determine the admission cost for a class field trip to include all students in the class and chaperones at a 4:1 student-to-chaperone ratio. Ask them to justify their answers.

Newspaper Sports Data

Have students find the data from a home team football game. Have them determine which quarterback had the best pass completion percentage. Ask them to explain how they determined the answer.

Sporting Goods Catalog or Sports Store Ad

Have students compare the cost of purchasing equipment for various sports. For which sport is equipment most expensive? Least expensive? Remind students to find the mean cost of a piece of equipment if several possibilities are available (e.g., the mean cost of a tennis racket or pair of ski boots). Have them create a table to help explain their results.

Recipes

Have students select a favorite recipe and determine the amount of each ingredient that would be needed to make enough to feed the entire class (or school). Have them explain how they figured out the ingredient amounts.

Nutritional Labels

Ask students to compare the sugar and fat content in ten different cereals or snack foods. Ask them to create a graph to show their findings and then to write about their observations, insights, and conclusions.

Too many possible discussion points will arise. We must skillfully sift through them to find the best ones for each lesson.

When our students have something to talk about, they are able to process new ideas, express wonderful math insights, and share the development of their thinking. Providing students with something to talk about through problem-based activities, manipulative tasks, children's literature, real-world data, and thoughtful questions challenges our students to think about math ideas and allows us to hear what is going on in their heads as they make sense of those ideas.

Questions for Discussion

1. What types of questions develop and refine students' thinking?

2. How might teachers sharpen their skills at asking thoughtful questions?

3. Ask a colleague to observe your math lesson and record the questions you ask. Analyze the types of questions you asked. What did you learn about your teaching?

4. In what ways do problem-based tasks stimulate communication?

5. Have your students shown an increased capacity to talk about math after working with manipulatives or hearing math-related stories? Explain your observations.

CHAPTER 3

Orchestrating Math Talk

Because many more ideas will come up than are fruitful to pursue at the moment, teachers must filter and direct the students' explorations by picking up on some points and by leaving others behind.

—National Council of Teachers of Mathematics,
Professional Standards for Teaching Mathematics

In Chapter 2, we discussed the role of teacher questioning in building student understanding. Thoughtful questions guide students' thinking and push students to clarify their understanding. Thoughtful questions hone students' listening skills and encourage student-to-student interactions. And thoughtful questions allow us to check for student understanding. Thoughtful questions prompt students to talk about math. We have acknowledged that we want to get students talking about math, but it can be challenging to manage that talk and ensure that it is focused and productive. While we want students to talk, we want to be sure they are talking about key math ideas and that their talk leads them to discoveries and insights. So how do we manage that talk to ensure it is beneficial to our students? Throughout this chapter we explore varied formats for talk in the math classroom, ranging from whole-class discussions to small teacher-led groups to cooperative learning groups to partner work and one-on-one discussions. Selecting the appropriate format from these varied possibilities allows us flexibility in choosing one that suits our needs and promotes productive talk.

The Value of Whole-Class Discussions

We often grumble about how little time we have to teach the many skills and concepts in our mathematics curriculum. We are pressured to find ways to teach math more quickly, and it is easy to see why some teachers may conclude that telling students the key ideas is quicker than having them explore the ideas on their own. The sense is that teaching to the whole class is quicker and more efficient, and yet, do we really believe that is true? Do we know what is going on inside students' heads when we are "telling" them about math? Could they be thinking about the television show they saw last night? Or are they anticipating the basketball game later tonight? One of the disadvantages of whole-class instruction is that students can disappear within the class. They can nod their heads and appear to be listening and understanding, only to have us discover while reviewing their work that they missed key math ideas.

Posing frequent questions during whole-class instruction is an effective way to keep students involved in learning math. Frequently asking questions can transform a "lecture" into an interactive experience. Questions pull daydreaming students back into the lesson and guide them to think about the math. Questions can help us monitor understanding, so we are not surprised at misunderstandings at the end of the lesson. Questions can promote student-to-student discussions, prompting students to think about and elaborate on each other's ideas. Rather than giving a lecture about math content during which students may, or may not, be tuned in to our words, making questions a regular part of whole-class instruction engages students and allows them to learn through our words, their own words, and the words of their classmates.

Using techniques like the think-pair-share (Kagan 1992) strategy discussed in Chapter 1, or simply asking students to "turn and share" with the person sitting next to them, will allow us to move back and forth between whole-class and partner discussions. Teachers who ask frequent questions and use pairing techniques are maximizing their whole-class instruction to allow for ongoing communication for their students.

Talk in Small Teacher-led Groups

We recognize that students do not come to us at the same skill level or with the same amount of prior knowledge. There are times when whole-class lessons may be ineffective because of the varied levels of the learners. Often we choose to specifically address the needs of a small group of learners, knowing that they might need to hear the content in a different way or have increased opportunities to talk with us about the ideas. Small teacher-led groups are a way to differentiate our instruction to meet the needs of struggling students or high-achieving students. Perhaps one group of students needs to hear a concept again or needs to be supported as they do a problem, so we can model ideas through think-alouds and ask questions to prompt their understanding, while others in the class work alone on an assignment or work in small groups to complete a task. This format provides us an opportunity for additional modeling and allows us to have teacher-to-student discussions with a smaller student-to-teacher ratio. In addition, small-group discussions can allow us to challenge our advanced students by bringing up more complex ideas or posing more difficult tasks.

Certainly the biggest challenge in conducting small teacher-led groups is the management of the other students in the classroom while our attention is with one small group. Taking the time to get all students started on their independent task prior to beginning our small group is critical, including walking through the room to ensure that students are focused and engaged. Clearly explaining all assignments and having a student restate the directions to be sure they were clear can prevent later problems. Recording the assignment on the board provides a visual reference for students, and having an "If you get finished early" task is necessary. Being sure that the students who are not in your small group understand your expectations for them is essential (i.e., Can they talk? Can they walk around the room? Where do they put their assignment when they are done? What do they do if they don't know an answer or how to proceed on an assignment?) The answers to those questions will depend on your preferences and your style, but be sure your students know your answers.

Small teacher-led groups provide students with opportunities to talk about math ideas at their level. These groups are formed as needed based on your students' understanding of a specific skill or concept. A pre-assessment may indicate that some students already know a skill and can be challenged with more complex tasks. A homework or class assignment may indicate that a group of students did not understand a skill and would benefit from additional review and further discussion of the ideas. These groups are not static, but change with the needs of your students. While they require attention to specific classroom management concerns (e.g., ensuring that all students within the class are engaged in constructive math work), these small groups are extremely effective at meeting the needs of varied levels of students by allowing them opportunities for math talk in a teacher-directed, small-group setting.

Student-to-Student Talk in Cooperative Groups

In addition to learning from teacher-led discussions, it is important for students to have opportunities to communicate with peers in a non-teacher-directed format. Cooperative learning groups, which are groups of students working together to perform a task, allow students to manage their own talk as they explore math ideas. When students are involved in cooperative learning tasks, the teacher's role changes. We have less direct control over each group's talk, but we continue to listen to student discussions, check for understanding, pose questions to guide thinking, and redirect those who are off-task. So, how do we ensure that the talk in cooperative groups is productive?

Stating the group task clearly and reviewing group expectations are critical to the success of cooperative group activities. Prior to students beginning their group task, they must clearly understand their assignment. Knowing the specific details is the critical piece to their ability to complete the task on their own and without confusion. What materials can they use? Where should they record their solution? Must they write a justification or explanation? How much time will they have to complete the task? Clearly explaining all facets of the task will ensure smooth group work. In addition, students must understand each person's role in ensuring that the task is completed. Your students may be able to divide responsibilities on their own, but many teachers have seen the benefits of assigning group roles (e.g., leader, reader, recorder, materials manager, checker, and reporter) to ensure that all students have a role in the group project and clearly understand that role.

Keeping students on task is a concern for many teachers. If students are not focused on the task, then you have wasted this opportunity for students to explore the math ideas and discuss their insights. Constantly moving through the room to monitor students' progress is essential. Groups are often asked to evaluate their group work and assess the participation of all members (see the Team Reflection on the CD). This group evaluation process reminds students that their contributions and behaviors are being observed by others within their group. And individual accountability is essential. Completing the group task is important, but the goal is for students to learn from the experience, so posing a follow-up task to check for individual student understanding (i.e., a similar problem to be solved or a writing task asking students to tell about their insights) is important. See the Classroom-Tested Tips for answers to some frequently asked questions about managing group work.

Guiding students as they explore math ideas continues to be important even in small-group explorations. We continue to use questioning to guide groups and partners to discover new ideas or modify their understandings. While some questions prompt students to listen to each other or keep them focused on the task, others guide their insights by probing into the data being collected or the solution being shared.

Seventh-grade students were working in groups to conduct a probability investigation. Miss Maletic observed them jumping to a conclusion without looking at all of the data they had collected. She asked them to prove their initial answer and asked for data to show that it was a reasonable answer. As they looked back on their data to defend their answer, they discovered data they had not initially considered. Without telling the students that they had made a mistake, their teacher was able to guide them to discover their mistake through her questions.

In order to maintain student interest, there are many cooperative learning formats that work well in the math classroom. Following are some cooperative learning structures that promote student-to-student communication and provide wonderful opportunities to explore and discuss math ideas.

Group Projects

Having students work in teams to complete a math project or solve a math problem is a simple way to promote communication. Group problem solving pushes group members to share their interpretations of the problem, discuss possible strategies and solutions, and plan for sharing their results with the class. Or groups might be asked to complete a math project to explore specific math concepts such as designing a playground that has an area of sixty-four square feet but is not shaped like a square. As they talk about the task, and share their ideas for completing it, they are reviewing or extending their understanding of the concept of area.

Team Brainstorming

In team brainstorming, the teacher asks a question that has multiple responses and allows time for team members to share and record their ideas (see Figure 3–1). Prompts might include:

> Name a time when you might need to calculate a percentage.
> List some data that would be appropriate to display on a stem-and-leaf plot.
> List some polyhedrons.

Initially students write all of their ideas, but then revisit those ideas, eliminating any that are not consistent with the prompt and then selecting some key ideas to share with the class. This technique encourages communication and reflection about their ideas.

Carousel Brainstorming

Carousel brainstorming is a great way to engage all students in generating ideas about a topic. It can be used as a review strategy or to preview prior knowledge before beginning a math topic.

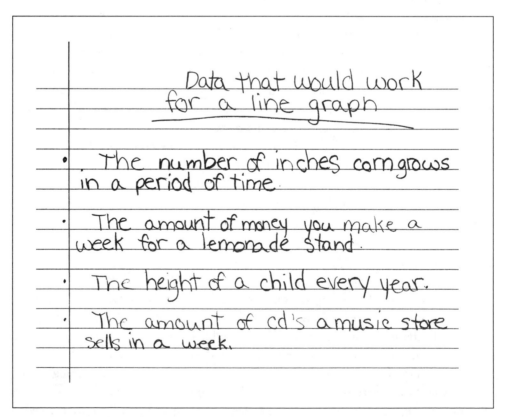

Figure 3–1 *Students compile a list of data that would be appropriate to display using a line graph.*

Chart paper is posted in five or six locations around the classroom, preferably spaced so the charts are not too close together and on various walls around the room. Each sheet has a math prompt for students to consider. Students are placed in groups and group recorders are given a marker. Providing a different-colored marker to each group leader will allow you to monitor each group's responses. Each group is asked to begin at a different piece of chart paper. The teacher explains the traffic flow, showing students how they are to move around the room from one piece of paper to the next. A timer is set. Students begin on their first prompt. When the timer rings, they move to the next paper and begin the next prompt, adding their answers to the ones that have already been recorded. Students continue to work through each station, moving each time the timer rings. When they return to their starting location, they are asked to review all of the recorded comments and select a few to report to the class. Prompts to get students talking about probability might include:

List examples of independent and dependent events.
List probability vocabulary.
List times when you might want to know the probability of an event.
List examples of unfair games.
List examples of equally likely events.

Through this carousel brainstorming activity, students have an opportunity to review a variety of probability ideas as they move from paper to paper and respond to the varied prompts. Since students work in groups, they are able to share ideas as they brainstorm with their team. This technique also allows for student movement, which can be helpful for some students who need to get up and move occasionally, and the timer signals students to continually move to new chart paper and focus on new prompts, keeping them engaged in the thinking process.

Numbered Heads

In Numbered Heads (Kagan 1992), students work in teams with each person assigned a number (e.g., 1, 2, 3, 4). The teacher poses a problem and students solve it as a team. After teams have solved and discussed the problem, the teacher calls a number and only that student can explain their team's solution. Not knowing who will represent their group in sharing the solution pushes teams to discuss the solutions and promotes tutoring for those team members who do not understand the answer or may not have been first to solve it. Rather than the same few students always reporting the answer to the teacher, students must share their ideas with their teammates to ensure that all team members are able to answer and explain the solution.

Talking Between Partners

Partner work is a quick, easy, and effective way to stimulate math talk. There is no need to move chairs or assign roles, and because of the ease of partner work as compared to group work, we are inclined to ask students to do it more frequently.

Partner talk might be very brief and can be interspersed throughout a lesson. In partner talk, more students are actually talking since there are only two participants in each discussion. And when more students are involved in talking about math, more students are involved in *thinking* about math.

Partner collaboration is a valuable way to have students check assignments (see Figure 3–2). Students might compare assignments to see if they have the same answers and then confer about any answers that differ, deciding on the correct answer together or signaling for the teacher if they cannot come to a resolution on their own. Partners might also team up to review math skills and ideas, with one student "asking" and one "answering" and then reversing roles.

Partner talk can be a good option for management reasons. While the noise level in the class may have to be monitored with so many voices talking at once, the periods of talk are generally briefer, so behavior problems tend to be minimal. There are fewer personalities to clash and less people to quibble over who is doing what. Some students who cannot handle working in larger groups are able to effectively share with just one other person.

While many partner talk opportunities are brief, partners are also an option for lengthier problem-solving tasks or projects. While there are fewer perspectives than when three or four students bring their knowledge to a task, partner discussions still challenge students to express their ideas, listen to someone else's ideas, and defend their strategies and solutions.

Figure 3–2 *These students collaborate to check the accuracy of their work.*

Managing Partner and Group Work

Managing group work can be challenging. We often get overwhelmed with the potential problems and decide that whole-group instruction would be less cumbersome, but the benefits of group work should prompt us to reconsider. Recognizing the potential pitfalls and planning for them will help minimize the disadvantages of the small-group format. The following are some typical teacher concerns with small-group work, as well as some insights and tips from classroom teachers who effectively use this format within their classrooms.

Problem	Possible Actions
One student in the group takes over to answer the question or complete the task.	There are some forceful students who like to take over the group. If you notice this happening within your room, try this . . . • Assign roles—for example, a leader, a recorder, and a reporter—so that each student has a role within the group. • Try a technique like Numbered Heads (Kagan 1992) in which each person in the group is assigned a different number (e.g., 1, 2, 3, or 4) with the teacher calling a number when it is time to share solutions. See more detailed description in Student-to-Student Talk in Cooperative Groups. • Give each student a paper clip to place in the center of the group after they share a possible answer. Students may not respond again until everyone's paper clip is in the center. Once all group members have shared an idea, students can pick up their paper clips and start over.
The group is off-task.	This will definitely happen—in fact, the further you are from a group, the better chance they are off-task—so . . . • Put on your comfortable shoes and keep moving throughout the room. • Do not sit at your desk or grade papers! Your attention must be on circulating through the room and keeping groups on-task. • Require students to record ideas as they work. Writing allows you to see what they are talking about and keeps them engaged and accountable.

Problem	Possible Actions
The small groups seem confused about the task or are proceeding incorrectly.	Class time is precious, and allowing students to continue when they are confused about the task will waste precious time, so . . . • Call a class time-out. Ask for all students to put down their pencils, stop talking, and look at you. Review the task, ask students to share a few ideas, and get groups jump-started with the assignment. Then, ask them to go back to their group work and carefully observe to be sure they are on target.
One student is not participating.	Some students like to try to disappear within the group, so . . . • Assign roles for each group member. • Consider using pairs rather than groups of three to four students. It is much harder to disappear in partner work!
The group is not moving through the task in a timely manner.	Students can often be on-task but spend too much time on one part of the project or another, so . . . • Set a timer. • Remind students of the amount of time remaining and what part of the task they should be working on (i.e., "Begin to summarize your strategy for solving the problem and start recording your ideas.").
The groups are getting very loud and there is too much movement in the room.	This is a judgment call. We all tolerate different levels of noise and movement, but when it gets to the point where you are uncomfortable, try this . . . • Establish a signal to notify students that they should be quiet and listen to you (e.g., flicker the lights, raise your hand). Tell students about your concerns (e.g., they are getting too loud, students are moving through room). Remind them of your expectations, and then send them back to their group work. • Cut out a green, yellow, and red circle to use as signals similar to green, yellow, and red traffic lights. Green is posted on the board when all is going well. When noise or movement is at a level for concern, post the yellow *caution* circle. This tells students to get their behavior under control. If they do, the green circle is reposted. If a red light appears, group work is stopped.

Problem	Possible Actions
	• Use consequences to send important messages to students. If group work is actually stopped because of behavior, students will be more compliant next time they are asked to adjust their behavior.
One student does not get along with the others in the group.	Consider student personalities when forming your groups so you can minimize the possibility of two clashing personalities. If it does happen, try this . . .
	• Encourage them to get along. Remind them of your behavior expectations.
	• Consider changing group members when you notice clashing personalities.
	• Have consequences for inappropriate group behaviors. Don't be afraid to remove a student from a group for the remainder of the task. Most students prefer working in groups rather than doing the task on their own. The next day, give them another chance to join a group, but when inappropriate behavior stops others from learning, remove the student from the group.
One person is incorrect, but is pushing his or her wrong answer on the others.	Some students can be quite forceful in their ideas, even when they are wrong! Try this . . .
	• Ask some questions to try to unveil the error.
	• Join the discussion, if needed, to help guide the debate or bolster the confidence of those who may quietly disagree.
	• Remind students that wrong answers are part of the process so that teasing or inappropriate remarks do not occur.
One group is finished with the task, but other groups are still working.	Groups finish at different speeds. So . . .
	• Always have a follow-up activity ready for speedy groups. Maybe it is a similar task with different data or just a question to discuss about the task (e.g., "Will that procedure always work? Can you find an example when it might not?").
There is just not enough time today to do group work!	Group work can take time, but there are so many benefits. Find ways to fit it in:
	• Try quick partner sharing rather than group projects.
	• Ask students to work in groups to briefly brainstorm ways to get started on a task, then assign the task as homework.

Problem	Possible Actions
	• Have students share solutions from homework or a previous assignment to compare their answers and discuss their strategies.
	• Be sure to fit in communication even if it must be for short periods of time. The benefits are too great to miss!

The Power of Presentations

While talking among groups and partners is a valuable way to explore math ideas, presenting those ideas to the class requires additional skills—students must summarize and clarify their learning in order to clearly express it to their classmates. Asking individuals, pairs, or groups to do class presentations is an important way to share insights and hone students' communication skills. It also provides accountability for group and partner tasks when students know that they will be required to report their ideas to others.

We agree that students learn when they hear others' ideas, but listening to classmates share their ideas can often be tedious. How do we help students present their ideas effectively? How do we help students learn to listen to others' ideas? If students cannot clearly present their ideas in a way that classmates can understand or are interested in hearing, then the time spent on the presentations has not been well used. To make the most of class presentations, some attention to presentation skills is helpful.

Demonstrate a presentation for your students. Model and share tips to support your students as they plan their own presentations. Would a visual help? Was it easier to understand when they saw some words, numbers, or pictures as you spoke? Maybe representations of the data would support their talk, or some notes on a piece of chart paper would remind them of important points to make. Students' presentations are most effective when classmates can both see and hear the ideas. Students might record key ideas on chart paper or share their representations on large sheets of construction paper. Have the materials (e.g., construction paper, chart paper, markers, overhead transparencies) available for students in a place where they are accessible to all teams.

Provide students with adequate time to plan their presentations, practice their talk, and complete their visuals. How many times have you watched students nervously stand waiting for their partner to speak? Offer students a chance to practice before they present to the class, to allow time to work out any kinks in their presentation. Remind students to face the class or have a designated spot in the room where presenters stand so everyone can see and hear them. Have a silent signal (e.g., touching your ear) to prompt presenters who are speaking too softly so you do not have to interrupt their presentation. Provide a time limit for presentations. How long should they speak? How much detail do you want to hear? It is generally preferable to encourage students to keep their presentations "short and to the point" to hold class-mates' interest.

Although developing presentation skills is important, developing listening skills is equally important. The goal is for classmates to hear each other's ideas and reflect on those ideas. To keep classmates tuned in to presentations, consider posing reflective questions following each presentation:

"What strategy did Kenny's group use to solve the problem?"
"What data led Tyler's group to that conclusion?"
"How was Mario's solution different from Jada's?"

After listening to a presentation, you might have students turn to a partner and develop a question related to the presentation content and then pose their questions to the class. Students might be encouraged to take simple notes during presentations to stay focused. Or you might ask students to construct brief written feedback for the presenters stating a fact they learned, a question they have, or a specific piece of praise.

I learned that . . .
I am wondering . . .
I liked when you . . .

Helping students become better listeners means helping them stay focused on the presentations and helping them absorb and reflect on the ideas.

Individual Teacher-to-Student Chats

One-on-one talks with our students do not have to be time-consuming and can easily fit into our schedules when skillfully done. They might be interviews about students' ideas or individual questioning to prompt their thinking or assess their understanding. These chats might take place during class activities, as other students are involved in an independent task or working in small groups. We might simply stop next to a student to talk or we might ask a student to come to our desk for an informal interview, maybe discussing an assignment, reading a journal entry together, or chatting about a concept just presented in class. This opportunity to talk one-on-one with a student provides him or her with individual support through scaffolded questions or repeated explanations and affords us a quick check of student understanding.

Differentiating Instruction Through Group and Partner Work

When students are involved in group work, we are able to effectively differentiate learning within the classroom. Students may all be working on the same problem with the teacher posing different questions as she moves from group to group, or students may be working on varied levels of a task or problem. For example, a class of sixth-grade students may be exploring area, but the students are at varied levels of their understanding. The teacher pairs students and poses one of the following tasks to each pair dependent on their current level of understanding:

Level 1: Partners are given tangrams and asked to create a triangle using 2 small triangles and one medium-sized triangle. They are asked to trace their design and then to determine the area of the design when one small triangle is one unit of area. The pair is asked to work together to justify their answer.

Level 2: Partners are given tangrams and asked to create two triangles of different sizes using at least 2 tans to make each triangle. They are asked to trace their triangles and then to determine the area of each one when one small triangle is one unit of area. The pair is asked to work together to justify their answers.

Level 3: Partners are given tangrams and asked to create as many triangles as possible using at least 2 tans for each one. They are asked to trace their triangles and then to determine the area of the triangles when one small triangle is one unit. The pair is asked to work together to justify their answers.

Having students work in groups allows us to pose varied tasks to better meet our students' needs while still providing all students with explorations related to the concept of *area*.

Along with group work, questions allow us to differentiate learning. Not all students will require, or benefit from, the same types of questions. We can use them to scaffold ideas for one group that needs support with foundational skills (e.g., "Can you tell me what *area* is? How will you find the area of your triangle?"), and use other questions to challenge those who are ready to move further in their thinking (e.g., "So could you create a quadrilateral that has the same area as your triangle?"). Our questions, as well as our selection of grouping formats, give us the flexibility to differentiate learning for groups within the same classroom.

C L A S S R O O M - T E S T E D   T I P

Student Surveys to Stimulate Communication

Students are always interested in data about themselves! Capitalize on this interest to stimulate discussions about data. Using a variety of creative surveys, students can be challenged to record data about themselves. Class data can then be the topic for discussions or writing projects.

Collecting the Data

Data collection does not have to be done during class time. Posting the question and graphic on a bulletin board or chalkboard allows students to record their data independently. Perhaps every Friday is your Data Day and students are routinely posed a question during their class warm-up time. The data are then available for use during class time.

Teachers might laminate charts or tables (see the customizable Student Survey Charts on the CD for some possibilities) and then use a wipeable, water-based (overhead transparency) pen to record the day's question. Wipeable pens can then be used by students to record their data. Using wipeable markers allows the teacher to simply erase the chart at the end of the class period and reuse it to gather data for the next class.

Stimulating Communication

Students might first be asked to discuss the data with a partner or group. Groups then report some of their observations to the class. Students should be encouraged to express data in multiple ways. When viewing the following data, for example, students might say:

Would you like to be on a TV reality show?	
Yes	No
卌 卌 卌 卌 IIII	卌 I

1. Twenty-four out of thirty people in our class would like to be on a reality show.

2. About $\frac{4}{5}$ of our class would like to be on a reality show.

3. About $\frac{1}{5}$ of our class doesn't want to be on a reality show.

4. The ratio of students in our class who want to be on it to the ones who don't is 4:1.

Students can be asked to write about the data with a partner or as an independent assignment. And be sure to ask students to analyze the data and make inferences or draw conclusions based on it. Do they think that people in the class want to be famous? Do they think their classmates are shy? Do they think their parents would answer this question the same way that they did?

Stimulating Independent Thinking

Begin with some easy polls, and then challenge students with more difficult surveys. Students might be polled about the following questions:

Are the Redskins going to win Sunday's football game? (yes or no)
Would you like a pet tarantula? (yes or no)

Do you like to read in bed? (yes or no)

What is your favorite meal of the day? (breakfast, lunch, or dinner)

Do you prefer chocolate, vanilla, or strawberry ice cream?

Do you like milkshakes, burgers, or both? (Record on a Venn diagram.)

Do you play soccer, basketball, or both? (Record on a Venn diagram.)

What is your favorite sport? (Give some choices.)

What is your favorite type of music? (Give some choices.)

How many hours did you sleep last night?

Find interesting questions that will motivate your students to talk math!

Examining Math Talk in Our Classrooms

How much math talk is going on in your classroom? We often focus on the challenges of writing about mathematics. But to be able to *write* about math, students need to *hear* math spoken and they need to have lots of opportunities to *talk* about their ideas. They need to hear your feedback as they verbalize their ideas. Did they clearly state their ideas? Do they need to be more specific? Did they leave out some important steps or ideas? Was there a better word to express what they were trying to say? As they practice communicating verbally, we have lots of opportunities to help them improve their understanding and their ability to communicate that understanding!

Take a few minutes to examine the math talk going on in your classroom. Think about the following questions:

What kinds of math talk happen in your classroom?

1. Do you talk about your own math thinking (think-alouds)?

2. Do you facilitate interactive whole-class discussions or small teacher-led group discussions?

   a. Do you ask students to explain their thinking?

   b. Do you ask "how," "why," and "what if"?

   c. Do you ask for reasons, proof, and math data to support answers?

   d. Do you encourage students to respond to each other?

   e. Do you use turn-and-share techniques to engage students in partner discussions in the midst of whole-class activities?

   f. Do you ask students to verbally summarize ideas at the end of a lesson as closure?

3. Do you encourage student-to-student talk through partner or small-group tasks?

   a. Do you design tasks that require students to give more than an answer? Do you push them to explain, describe, and justify their ideas?

   b. When students are working in groups, do you move through the room and engage in discussions with small groups of students?

   c. Do you encourage small groups or partners to share their ideas with the whole class?

4. Do you engage in math discussions with individual students (maybe quick conferences or interviews while others work on a class assignment)?

Questions for Discussion

1. Are students in your classroom talking about math on a regular basis? If not, what can you do to promote that communication?

2. All instructional formats have advantages and disadvantages. Think about whole-class lessons, small teacher-led groups, cooperative learning groups, and partner work. What are some advantages and disadvantages of each when focusing on improving math understanding? What are some advantages and disadvantages of each when focusing on improving math communication?

3. What are some concerns related to managing cooperative learning groups? How might you minimize problems during group work?

4. How can individual or group presentations benefit students, both the speakers and listeners? How might we help students listen better? How might we help them become better presenters?

Developing the Language of Math

If our students learn to do mathematics silently, they may find that they don't have words readily available to describe mathematical ideas.

—Rebecca Corwin, *Talking Mathematics: Supporting Children's Voices*

We recognize the value of students communicating about mathematics. Through communication, they formalize and share their ideas, discuss and extend their thinking, and provide us with critical assessment information. But what happens when students cannot find the words to express their math ideas? What happens when the language of mathematics prohibits them from communicating about the content of mathematics?

In order to communicate about any content area it is important to know the words that express that content. Without an understanding of content vocabulary, students are likely to get frustrated trying to share their ideas or to feel confused about the ideas shared by others. Words are the building blocks for content understanding. It is through words that we hear, read, and process our ideas. It is through words that we express and refine our understandings. Throughout this chapter, we explore vocabulary development as a critical tool for helping our students understand the math we are teaching and express their own math understandings.

The Challenges of Math Vocabulary

Vocabulary is important in all content areas, but in mathematics, vocabulary development is critical. The sheer volume of math vocabulary is staggering. Open any teacher's edition of a math textbook and you will find pages of math terms that affect your students' understanding of the concepts being taught. All of these words and terms can make mathematics quite confusing.

Math vocabulary is technical vocabulary. These words are not part of our conversations at the mall or around the dinner table. Students hear *congruent, isosceles, polygon,* and *equation* during math lessons, but they do not hear them outside of our classrooms. And to complicate the language even more, many math words have double meanings—an everyday meaning and a separate meaning in math. A *range* is not something you cook on and a *median* is not the strip in the middle of a highway. A *slope* does not refer to a hilly area, we don't sit at a math *table,* and *volume* is not how we control the sound on the television. Mastering the language of math can be a bit daunting.

Critical Components of Vocabulary Instruction

While we all remember being asked to look up words in a dictionary and copy the definitions, we also can remember copying the words without any thought to the actual meanings! If our goal is to help our students understand and use math words, we need to find ways to engage students in exploring word meanings. Teaching vocabulary is not about locating, or copying, formal dictionary definitions. A focus on math vocabulary means helping students internalize and use the words that help them understand and express math ideas.

Are you wondering, "When will I ever have time to do math vocabulary activities with all of the math content I have to teach?" This is a reasonable question if we view vocabulary activities as separate from activities that explore and teach math concepts. But what if we designed activities that addressed *both* content understanding and vocabulary development? Is it possible to weave vocabulary development into our math lessons? And could these "vocabulary activities" also enhance our students' understanding of math concepts? The key to effectively developing math vocabulary is to introduce and use math vocabulary in context. Providing a language-rich environment, and ensuring that vocabulary is appropriately introduced and revisited as a natural part of our lessons, will help our students grasp the language of mathematics. The key is to design activities that *both* help students explore math concepts *and* help them become familiar with the language of mathematics.

In designing classroom activities that support vocabulary development, some critical criteria include the following:

■ Frequent and repeated exposure to words—Students do not learn words after seeing or hearing them once. They need repeated opportunities to hear and use the words in various math contexts.

■ Engagement—Students learn when they are engaged. Activities that get them involved through group work, hands-on experiences, or engaging formats help them "tune-in" to the words and ideas of the lesson.

■ Discussions—We do not learn a language by listening to someone else speak it. Activities that get students talking about math help them continue to develop their communication and language skills.

■ Everyday language—Define new words using language that is familiar to your students, including examples and illustrations.

Vocabulary must be taught, but teaching does not imply telling the definition or having students look it up in the dictionary. Vocabulary activities that get students talking about math ideas, that help them understand new words using familiar words, and that provide repeated experiences with words benefit our students both in their vocabulary development and in their content understanding.

Building Vocabulary Through a Language-Rich Classroom

In Chapter 1, we talked about the importance of creating a language-rich environment. This is critical for vocabulary development. Students learn math words when they are immersed in the language of math. Provide lots of opportunities for your students to hear, see, and use math vocabulary. Consider these ways to immerse your students in the language of math:

■ Talk math. Model the use of appropriate math vocabulary as you explain and describe math processes.

■ Ask thoughtful questions that push students to use math words. Ask questions that need to be answered by more than yes, no, or a number. Ask students how and why, so they have opportunities to explain their mathematical thinking. Support them as they find the best words to express what they are trying to say.

■ Elicit multiple responses. When asking for a response from students, don't stop after one student's response. Ask several other students to share their answers. Students need to hear ideas expressed in lots of different ways! When necessary, prompt students to find the appropriate words to express their idea.

■ Encourage group work. Frequent cooperative learning activities provide students with the opportunity to hear others' ideas and vocabulary. The activity might be as simple as to turn and share an idea with a partner.

■ Share what you hear. As you walk through the room monitoring group or partner activities, listen for interesting vocabulary to share. Share some of the things you hear (i.e., "In this group I heard someone say . . ." "Group 2 had an interesting way to describe . . .").

■ Post math words in the classroom. Build a word wall with your students to highlight key vocabulary. Frequently reference the wall to discuss the words and meanings.

■ Write it. Ask students to write about their math thinking. Model writing for your students. Brainstorm some key words prior to writing to focus students' ideas and support them with key vocabulary.

■ Provide lots of feedback! Provide students with specific feedback regarding the words they use to express their math ideas. Share alternate words that might help students "get to the point." Celebrate word choices! Praise students for using appropriate math words. Encourage them to take risks as they try to find the best words to express their ideas.

Introducing Math Vocabulary

In the middle grades, students continue to experience many new math words. Specifically introducing this new math vocabulary provides a foundation for students' understanding of the concepts. Research studies (Marzano, Pickering, and Pollock 2001) have shown the benefits of vocabulary instruction on the comprehension of new content. Introducing new math words and allowing students time to process and explore those words supports their understanding of the math ideas and provides them with the language to communicate about those ideas.

Using understandable vocabulary is critical when introducing new words. If our students do not know what a *parallelogram* is and we employ a "look it up in the dictionary" approach, consider what they will find:

A quadrilateral with parallel and congruent opposite sides

Clear enough? Will our students understand that definition? Math vocabulary is technical vocabulary, and technical vocabulary is often defined using other technical vocabulary. Students must be able to understand our definitions. Along with simple, understandable language, the use of examples and illustrations will serve to clarify our introductions (e.g., pictures or models of parallelograms), and making connections to previously learned words and concepts helps students construct meaning for the new word (i.e., the concepts of *parallel* and *congruent*).

Introducing new words in context is the optimal way to support vocabulary development. While students describe math ideas in the best way they can, we can capitalize on certain classroom moments to interject the specific math terms. As students mention the *sides* of the right triangle, we might paraphrase their ideas by replacing the word *sides* with the more specific words *legs* or *hypotenuse*.

STUDENT:, That side is 5 centimeters long.
TEACHER: So you are saying that the hypotenuse, the side across from the right angle, is five centimeters long? (pointing to the hypotenuse and right angle on the diagram on the board)

As students talk about the *answer*, we might paraphrase their response using the words *product* or *quotient*, providing continued opportunities for students to hear appropriate math vocabulary.

STUDENT: The *real probability* of rolling a prime number is 3/6, but when we did it we got about 2/6.

TEACHER: So the results of your experiment didn't match the *theoretical probability*, what you thought should happen mathematically?

STUDENT: No, it should have been 3/6.

TEACHER: Explain your thinking to me.

STUDENT: There are 6 numbers on a die, but just 2, 3, and 5 are prime, so you get the *real probability* by saying 3/6 or you could say 1/2.

TEACHER: So because there are 3 prime numbers and 6 numbers on the die, your *theoretical probability* is 3/6?

(*Students nod.*)

TEACHER: But your *experimental probability*, what happened when you tried it, didn't match that?

In this brief give-and-take the teacher attended to both language and concepts. Sharing specific terms at the point of use and in a nonjudgmental way will help students clarify and enhance their use of math vocabulary.

Not all words will surface spontaneously in classroom conversation. The introduction of math vocabulary requires us to make some instructional decisions. Which words should we introduce? How should we introduce them? There are many vocabulary words in math, so it may be necessary to select those we want to formally introduce to students. Our textbooks or curricula often highlight key words, but the best way to determine which words to introduce is to consider your math standards and select those words that are critical to understanding and communicating about the content you are addressing. What words would you use if you were talking about line graphs? Might you use the words *title, label, axis, interval,* or *scale*? Select those words that are critical to your content, and then introduce them just a few at a time, being sure to use language that is understood by your students, visuals and examples to help them grasp the ideas, and connections to words and ideas that they already know. We might introduce *reflection* by demonstrations using an overhead projector or video visualizer, sketching pictures on the board, relating it to rotations, and explaining it using the more familiar term *flip*. After our discussion, writing the word clearly on a sentence strip and posting it on the classroom wall (our beginning of a math word wall) will provide ongoing support as students begin to familiarize themselves with the term (and the concept). When introducing *translations*, we might repeat a similar process but this time make connections with the concept of *reflection* and the more primary word *slide*. Each word (and concept) builds on another. But were we teaching the vocabulary or the concept of *reflections* and *translations*? Through language-based experiences, using words, pictures, and examples to illustrate the concept, we are able to teach both.

Word Walls

Although discussions about vocabulary are critical, seeing the words in a written format is also important for students as they learn new words. Word walls are visual displays of critical content vocabulary. They are not merely bulletin boards, but are instructional tools that are built, or constructed, collaboratively with students. These organized word displays are posted on a classroom wall or bulletin board to provide opportunities for students to see and reference key words. In classrooms that effectively use word walls, students can often be seen turning to the word wall during class discussions to find just the right word to express their ideas, or referencing the word wall during independent writing activities to support their selection of words. When built collaboratively with students, word walls allow students to visualize words, see connections between words, and explore word meanings.

The physical characteristics of the word wall are critical to making it a functional tool. Posted words should be large enough, and written boldly enough, for all students to see from any part of the room. If there is not enough wall space, word walls can be created on cabinets, rolling carts, cardboard tri-folds, or whiteboards. Word walls may include math symbols. Organizing words by math content standard (e.g., geometry, algebra, measurement) or math topic (e.g., percents, ratios, triangles) allows students to view clusters of words that connect to each other and a particular math concept. Keep in mind, however, that a word (e.g., *scale*) may connect to several math concepts (i.e., *scale* as a tool to measure weight or as a component of a graph), so duplicate words may occur when clustering by standard or concept, but duplicate words will remind students of the dual meanings for some math terms.

Words should be introduced gradually. Word walls are built interactively with students. You might write the new word on chart paper, a sentence strip, or a paper "brick" to build your "wall." The word may be used in a sentence or students might be asked to brainstorm the meaning of the word. As each word is introduced, discuss the word as it relates to other known math words or concepts and then place it in an appropriate spot on the wall. Including illustrations associated with the word is also a support for many students who better retain words associated with graphic images. You might draw an equilateral triangle next to the word *equilateral* or a percent sign by *percent*. Take advantage of any opportunity to connect words to visual images and math symbols. This is of special importance to English language learners (ELL) or students with language difficulties.

Word walls enhance our introduction of new vocabulary by allowing us to show each word in print, and they provide an ongoing resource for our students as they write and talk about mathematics. The more our students examine the word walls, through ongoing classroom activities that direct their attention to the words, the more familiar they will become with the words. See the Classroom-Tested Tips for a variety of quick and easy ideas for keeping students tuned in to the words on your word wall.

CLASSROOM-TESTED TIP

Word Wall Fun

When you find yourself with a brief period of time (i.e., a few quick minutes before class is over), try turning your word wall into an instructional activity.

■ Give a clue, then ask students to find the word that goes with your clue.

■ Ask students to find two words on the wall that go together (are connected in some way) and to justify their answers (i.e., *trapezoid* and *rhombus* are both quadrilaterals, *legs* and *hypotenuse* are both names for sides of a right angle).

■ Select a word and ask students to work with a partner to create a quick web of all the words they can think of that connect to that word (concept). (Word webs are discussed later in this chapter.)

■ Ask students to define a word or use the word in a sentence to show their understanding.

■ Ask students to draw pictures or act out their understanding of a word on the wall.

■ Share a topic with the class (e.g., box-and-whisker plots) and ask students to find all of the words on the wall that connect to your topic.

Provide students with varied opportunities to interact with the words on the wall. It will build their understanding and confidence in using the words.

Vocabulary Logs

There is great value in having students record ideas. When we write ideas, we make them our own. During the introduction of math vocabulary, having students record the new words, and their understanding of the meanings of the words, will help them process the ideas and better remember the words and meanings.

Vocabulary logs are one way for students to record new math words. Following classroom discussions to develop word meanings, you might ask students to record the new word and its definition (in their own words) in their vocabulary log (see Figure 4–1). Students are encouraged to include illustrations or examples to help them remember the meaning of each word. As students record their words and definitions, the teacher circulates through the room to be sure that the definitions are appropriate.

Vocabulary logs might be a bound book (e.g., a marble composition book) or might simply be a designated section of a loose-leaf binder. The look of the log is less important than the functions it provides—to allow students to record and process their ideas about new words and concepts and to provide a ready reference for students who might need to search for a word or meaning. These logs extend vocabulary support outside the classroom as students are encouraged to take them home for reference while doing homework assignments. And vocabulary logs allow students to find words from previous lessons, even when those words may have been replaced by new ones on the classroom word wall—one of the dilemmas of so many vocabulary words being introduced throughout the school year.

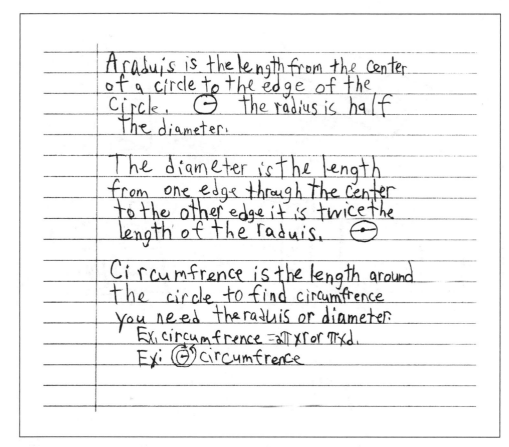

Figure 4–1 *This student records his understanding of radius, diameter, and circumference using words and pictures.*

Foldable Study Guides

Another practical and engaging way for students to record their understandings about math words is through the creation of foldable study guides. By simply folding paper, students can create study guides to record words, definitions, illustrations, and/or examples. The guides might be kept in a two-pocket folder or a binder folder and can be a handy reference for in-class or homework assignments.

Students might fold a sheet of paper in half and record their understanding of prime and composite numbers, fold it in thirds and describe isosceles, equilateral, and scalene triangles, or fold it in fourths and record their understanding of commutative, associative, distributive, and identity properties (see the ideas shown in Figure 4–2). Creating study guides challenges students to express their understanding of key words and concepts. Encourage them to use examples (or nonexamples) and pictures to help them show their thinking. Students love recording their understanding of vocabulary words in this creative way.

Word Boxes

Word boxes challenge students to share their understanding of a word in a variety of ways. Students are given a math word that they record in the center of the word box.

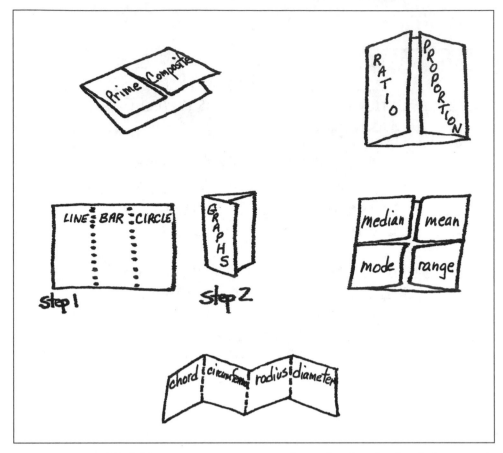

Figure 4-2 *Simply folding paper can create study guides that display definitions, pictures, and examples.*

Students then complete each box to show their understanding of the highlighted word (see Figure 4–3). The sections of the box might ask students to define, illustrate, provide examples and/or nonexamples, write word problems, or list related words. Students might work alone or in groups to complete their word box.

Variation: Rather than using the word box template, have students fold a piece of paper into four sections and tell them (or indicate with a template on the blackboard) what should be recorded in each section. If time is limited, have students fold their papers in two or three sections and select just two or three ways (e.g. define, illustrate, list related words) for the students to show their understanding of the word.

Using Word Origins to Promote Understanding

Knowledge of word origins can be a valuable tool in understanding math words. You may want to help your students recognize word prefixes and suffixes that give clues to meaning. Provide some word origin information to students and ask them to brainstorm math words that may be derived from those origins. Some common origins include the following:

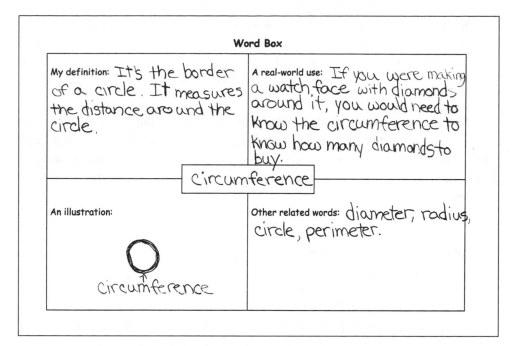

Figure 4–3 *This student shows her understanding of circumference through her responses to the varied prompts in the word box.*

$\frac{1}{2}$ – semi (Latin)	$\frac{1}{2}$ – hemi (Greek)
1 – uni (Latin)	1 – mono (Greek)
2 – bi (Latin)	2 – di (Greek)
3 – tri (Latin)	3 – tri (Greek)
4 – quadra (Latin)	4 – tetra (Greek)
quart (Latin)	
5 – quintus (Latin)	5 – penta (Greek)
10 – deci (Latin)	10 – deca (Greek)
100 – centi (Latin)	100 – hecto (Greek)
1000 – milli (Latin)	1000 – kilo (Greek)
equal – aequus (Latin)	equal – isos (Greek)

Exploring Double Meanings

Many math words have a math meaning and another meaning when used in everyday conversation. When these words appear in our math curriculum, they can confuse students. Some attention to the double meanings will help our students clarify the different uses of the words. When a new math word is introduced that has a different everyday connotation, acknowledging the different meanings will help eliminate confusion.

TEACHER: Today we are going to talk about volume. Does anyone know what volume is?

STUDENT: It is how you turn up the TV sound.

TEACHER: We do use that term to refer to the sound on a TV or radio, but today we are going to talk about volume related to math measurement, and it doesn't have anything to do with sound—same word, but a different meaning.

The teacher acknowledged students' everyday understanding of the word. She also acknowledged that they would be talking about the same word but then began to explore the new math meaning of *volume*. Students will be less confused if they have opportunities to talk about what they currently understand about a word and then move on to the new meaning.

Have some fun brainstorming the different meanings for math words. Provide your students with a list of words that have double meanings (a math meaning and an everyday meaning). Have them work with partners to record their understandings on a chart like the one in Figure 4–4.

Reviewing and Expanding Math Vocabulary

Introducing math words is critical, but finding ways to continue to review those words is equally critical. Repeated exposure to words is what helps students internalize those words. Try some of these activities to get your students using math words, and at the same time, discussing math ideas. Have fun and make your math classroom a language-rich classroom!

Word/Concept Webs

Word webs push students to brainstorm connections between words and in doing so, help them examine connections between math concepts. To begin students on a web, select a word or phrase (e.g., *geometry*, *measurement*, *polygons*, or *metric system*) and ask students to write the word or phrase in the center of their paper. Students then work in groups to brainstorm and record related words. For *metric system*, students

Word	It usually means . . .	In math it means . . .
mean		
median		
plane		
power		
rate		
right		
translation		

Figure 4–4 *Students can use a chart like this one to record the math meanings and everyday meanings of words.*

might record: *measurement, meter, liter, centimeter,* or *kilometer.* Once students have some time to generate words in their small groups, begin a class word web on a piece of chart paper or on the board. Ask students to share possible words for the class web. As words are shared, ask students to justify why each word belongs on the web and how it is related to the center word. Help students make connections between words by asking them to suggest where each word might be placed on the web (i.e., Are there any similar words that might go together?). These classroom discussions provide your students with repeated exposure to both the vocabulary words and the math concepts. You might ask students to reorganize their own webs based on how each word connects to the center word (i.e., metric system words might be organized based on whether they relate to distance or mass or capacity). Word webs are a great way to review vocabulary and assess students' conceptual understanding.

Math Vocabulary Bingo

Give each student a blank bingo card (see the templates on the CD). Provide each student with a list of words and ask students to write a word in each space (wherever they choose on their bingo card). After students have completed their bingo cards, it's time to play! Read a definition or description of the word (concept) and have students place a chip/marker on the correct word on their card. Students call *BINGO* when they have covered a row horizontally, diagonally, or vertically. Some variations might include:

- Show a picture to illustrate the word or phrase and have students cover the word that matches the picture clue (e.g., right triangle, parallelogram).

- For homework, have students create clues for a math bingo game based on the content they are studying in class.

- Have students work with a partner and use the glossary in their math book to come up with words and clues for a bingo game.

- Play partner bingo. Two students work together with one bingo card. The teacher reads a clue, definition, or description and the students talk it over and then cover the word on which they agreed. When a pair has bingo, they must work together to give the meaning of each word in order to claim their prize.

- Play special bingo games like *right angle bingo* in which students cover squares that form a right angle in order to call "bingo". Other possibilities might be *parallel bingo, perpendicular bingo, vertical bingo, horizontal bingo,* or *square bingo.*

Word Sorts

Sorting words will get your students talking about the words and their meanings. Select some important vocabulary words related to a math topic (e.g., *sides, angles, parallel, right angle, circle, square, rectangle, pentagon, quadrilateral, parallelogram, trapezoid*). Create a set of word cards and ask students to work in teams of four to sort them based on their math meanings. Ask each team to decide on a title or label for each group of words to explain why they belong together. Working in teams allows students to combine their ideas to discover a reasonable way to group the words. And even those students who do not understand the words will benefit from hearing the group conversations. After teams sort and label the words, have them explain their groupings to the class, justifying why they placed certain words in each group (see Figure 4–5). Teams will not all sort the words in the same way, but the process of sorting will generate discussion about the words and ideas. Through group presentations, students will see and hear different ways to sort and label the words and will expand their understandings of the words and concepts.

Word Match-Ups

Prior to lessons, it is helpful to review lesson vocabulary so students are reminded of key words and ready to discuss key ideas. Word match-ups are one way to provide

Figure 4–5 *This student explains how his team sorted the geometry vocabulary.*

that quick review. Write each vocabulary word on a sentence strip and then record brief definitions, in understandable words, on separate strips. Post the word strips on one side of the board and definition strips on the other side and then ask students to talk with a partner to find a word and definition that match. Ask partners to share their ideas. When an appropriate match-up is given, post the word next to the definition, and have students search for another. Having students discuss decisions with a partner gives them opportunities to talk the language of math and provides some quick tutoring for students who may be confused about the vocabulary. Continue until all of the words are matched with definitions.

Riddles

Riddles provide an engaging way to explore word meanings. You might create vocabulary riddles for students to solve or have students work with partners to write riddles for the class to solve.

> I am a prism.
> I have six sides.
> My faces are congruent squares.
> What am I?

Consider combining the writing of riddles with bingo to play Riddle Bingo. Decide on nine words for the bingo game. Divide the class into nine groups, with each group writing a riddle for one of the words. As each group reads their riddle, students must cover the word that solves that riddle.

Analogies

Analogies require students to think about words and the relationship between the words. Consider posing simple analogies to your students. Have students complete the analogies and justify their answers, or have them create analogies of their own.

> Product is to multiplication as _____ is to division.
> 90 degrees is to right angle as _____ is to straight angle.

The Language of Algebra

The language of mathematics contains complex vocabulary and complicated symbols. Students must understand the symbols of math in order to effectively speak the language of math, especially in the study of algebra. Talking about algebra challenges students to state math ideas both in words and in symbols. Provide students with math word phrases and challenge them to say the same thing using numbers and math symbols or vice versa (see Figure 4–6).

In words	In symbols and numbers
The sum of four and eight	$4 + 8$
The difference of 16 and 5	$16 - 5$
Two times the sum of five and seven	$2(5 + 7)$
One fourth of 16	$\frac{1}{4}(16)$
Three less than the sum of six and two	$(6 + 2) - 3$

Figure 4–6 *Students show their understanding of algebra vocabulary.*

For students to effectively communicate about math operations and effectively use equations to solve problems, it is important that they understand how to move from words to symbolic representations.

Eliminate It!

Provide students with four vocabulary words (e.g., *trapezoid, rhombus, pentagon, parallelogram*) and ask them to cross out, or eliminate, the word that does not belong with the others, justifying their choice.

trapezoid	rhombus
~~pentagon~~	parallelogram

"I eliminated pentagon *because it has five sides and the others are all quadrilaterals with four sides."*

Students are then asked to record the three words that go together and add a fourth word that belongs with the others, again justifying their decision.

trapezoid	rhombus
rectangle	parallelogram

"I added rectangle *because it has four sides like the others."*

Finally, students should decide on a title or label for the group of words (e.g., *quadrilaterals*).

Working with partners will ensure that students talk about the words and their meanings. Not all students will eliminate the same word, but asking students to justify their decisions will allow you to assess whether they understand the words and their meanings. (See the template for Eliminate It! on the CD.)

Interactive Word Play

Developing vocabulary should be an interactive pursuit, not a quiet task of copying words and definitions. Students become familiar with words as they use them and hear them being used. Group and partner activities are perfect for helping students internalize the language of math. For a fun partner activity, provide a set of index cards, with one vocabulary word on each card. Have one student pick a card and, without looking at the word, hold it to his or her forehead with the word facing his or her partner. The partner gives clues until the person holding the card is able to correctly identify the word. (This also works as a whole-class activity with the teacher holding a card to her forehead and students giving clues until she can figure out which word is on the card.) Whether you are playing as a whole class or students are playing in pairs, they will be enthused, active, and engaged with the words.

C L A S S R O O M - T E S T E D   T I P

Be Ready to Record

Have sentence strips and a thick marker within reach during math lessons. As key words arise in conversations, take a minute to record the word, talk about the word, and post the word on your word wall. Seize the opportunity to expand students' math vocabulary.

The Power of Words

Words are the building blocks of language. For students to effectively talk and write about math ideas they must be able to find the words to share those ideas. But helping students internalize the language of mathematics is not about dictionary definitions. Classroom activities that provide rich opportunities for math talk and teachers who introduce new math vocabulary using familiar language, illustrations, and examples help students better understand both the words of mathematics and the ideas of mathematics. Through specific attention to the development of students' math vocabularies, we can strengthen our students' understanding of math content and provide them with a critical tool for communicating about that content.

Questions for Discussion

1. How can attention to math vocabulary benefit students?

2. How might you introduce new math words?

3. How might you provide repeated exposure to words?

4. How might attention to math vocabulary support English language learners or students with low reading levels or language difficulties?

Writing to Learn and Learning to Write

It is important to give students experiences that help them appreciate the power and precision of mathematical language.

—National Council of Teachers of Mathematics,
Principles and Standards for School Mathematics

What does writing have to do with mathematics? Many of us cannot remember writing in math class. Math was about facts and figures, nothing that needed to be expressed in sentences or paragraphs. But as we have reevaluated our goals in mathematics and have shifted our focus from rote computations to understanding skills and concepts, we have recognized the important role that writing can—and should—play in our math classrooms. Math is not just about facts and figures; it is also about reasoning and conjecture and understanding.

What does writing have to do with mathematics? Writing is a process through which we record our observations, our thoughts, and our insights. It is a process through which we reorganize our ideas, develop conjectures, and gain insights. It is not content in itself, but a means of exploring and expressing content. So why would we *not* write in math class? We would certainly benefit from a tool to help us explore math processes. We would benefit from a vehicle for sharing our thoughts, insights, and beliefs about mathematics. In this chapter we explore the critical role of writing as an instructional tool to enhance and express student understanding.

The Benefits of Writing About Math

In Chapter 1, we discussed the many benefits of math communication for students and teachers. Both talk and writing get students actively involved in the learning process. Communicating about math ideas pushes students to organize their thoughts, helps them recognize confusions, and motivates them to dig deeper into their understanding. As teachers, we gain insight into students' knowledge and skills, are able to monitor their understandings and attitudes about math, and receive feedback that can help us to evaluate and improve our lessons. These benefits are true for both oral and written communication, but written communication has some additional benefits, including the following:

- Providing a permanent record of students' ideas to which they can later refer

- Spurring student discovery and insights by allowing them to view data and observations they have recorded

- Physically engaging students, making them active participants in a lesson

- Allowing us to monitor their thinking as we observe their writing, a reflection of their thinking.

- Helping us identify struggling students so that we can offer support.

- Pushing students to process and retain ideas as they take notes from a chapter they have read or summarize a concept they have been studying

- Enabling us to revisit students' ideas at a later date or possibly use their writing as a reference point during student or parent conferences

Before we can write about something, we need to know what we are thinking. While we can sometimes get by with quick oral responses and mask our lack of understanding, writing pushes us to examine those understandings in order to put our thoughts into words. We must identify and organize our thinking. And we are able to revise and modify our writing as we revise and modify our thinking. It is not easy, but it is an invaluable process as we explore content understanding. When we are able to write about an idea, we truly have internalized the idea. Our hope is for our students to cultivate a deep understanding of mathematics that can be developed and affirmed through writing.

The Challenges of Writing About Math

There is no doubt that many of our students have difficulty writing about math. It is not an easy task. But that does not mean we should allow students to simply provide us with computational answers without evidence of their thinking. We have students who have strong written language skills and struggle with computations, but rather than exempt them from the computation tasks, we support them in their area of weakness. If our students' area of weakness is written language, we are challenged to find ways to enhance their skills so they can both "do the math" and "explain the math they are doing." Being able to communicate about content is an important objective regardless of the content being studied (see Figure 5–1). Communication allows students to better explore math ideas and leads to many discoveries, and communication gives students the power to convey their ideas to others. It is a critical part of all learning.

Difficulties with writing about math are not solely determined by our students' abilities to write. Writing can be a painstaking task because it requires us to record our thoughts. And while recording thoughts may be easy when we are writing about what we did on our summer vacation, it is not so easy when we are asked to record our thoughts about a complex new math skill that we are learning. The content of mathematics can test even confident writers.

Our challenge in supporting our students as they write in math lies in the fact that they struggle for a variety of reasons. Some students struggle because they are unable to find the words to express their math ideas. Others struggle because they have difficulties with written language skills. Still others struggle because they are unsure or unclear about the mathematics concepts. Writing about math is difficult for students because it requires both process skills (e.g., language and writing skills) and content knowledge (e.g., math knowledge). Our goal is to support our students with the development of both process and content.

Figure 5–1 *Writing helps students process their ideas and extend their understanding.*

A Blend of Content and Process

When exploring writing in mathematics it is important to address both writing to learn and learning to write. Writing is a tool to help us delve into topics and explore ideas. Writing facilitates learning. But writing is not easy, and we must assist students with learning to write about mathematics. There are many tips we can share and strategies we can teach to help our students more effectively write about math content.

Whose job is it to teach writing, and when should it be taught? Students learn writing techniques in language arts classes. They learn to write for a variety of purposes, in a variety of formats, to a variety of audiences, and on a variety of topics. In math class, students have opportunities to apply what they are learning in their language arts classes to real situations as they write about math ideas. Is it easy? Definitely not! Do they struggle? In many ways! In order to effectively write about mathematics, our students must know mathematics and know how to write. Both mathematics teachers and language arts teachers can support students as they blend their content knowledge and writing skills.

A Word About Scoring

A variety of writing tasks are posed to middle grades students, pushing them to apply skills they are learning in language arts classes. Students might be asked to record observations, to display ideas on graphic organizers, to answer brief constructed response questions, or to engage in extended writing tasks. Each of these varied formats requires different writing skills as students attempt to record their thinking in appropriate and understandable ways. As we begin this discussion of writing in mathematics, it is important to clarify our own goals so that we are better able to appropriately guide and assess our students' writing. Is the writing task designed to stimulate student understanding of a math concept? If so, should it be scored for content or for language? Is the writing task designed to help students express their math ideas? Then should it be scored for clarity of thought as well as the math being conveyed? In Chapter 8, we discuss assessment in detail, but as we begin focusing on writing tasks it is important to keep our goals for each task in mind. It will not be necessary to grade each task. Some writing is developmental writing, a way of providing practice in getting ideas on paper. Other writing will be scored simply for the math content that is being conveyed, with writing simply being a tool that allows us to better glimpse students' thoughts. And still other tasks may be scored for both math and language skills when revision time is provided to allow students to apply their language arts skills.

Writing for Different Purposes

Writing serves a variety of purposes. At times we ask students to record their ideas simply to help them formalize them, to get them out of their heads and onto the paper so they can see and revise them. At other times, we want students to explain how they solved a problem so we can assess the appropriateness of their strategy, or we might ask students to describe a concept so we can help them identify their understanding of that concept. We might ask them to compare two concepts in order to deepen their understanding of both, or we might ask students to reflect on their thinking to be sure they have internalized important ideas. The varied writing tasks that we pose have varied benefits. Choosing just the "write" task ensures that students' thinking is challenged, and finding ways to support students as they engage in varied writing tasks builds their confidence and success.

Writing in mathematics should be focused on our math standards. Writing is simply the vehicle to push students' thinking and to allow us to assess their understanding. When asking students to write about math, we have many options in the prompts we might pose. The goal is to match the writing task with our intended outcomes. Following are some types of writing that support math content:

Type of Writing	Sample Prompts
Explain a Process	Explain how you got your answer.
Generalize or Draw Conclusions	What conclusions can you draw?
Justify an Answer or Process	Why do you believe that is the answer?
Create Word Problems	Write a story problem for $5x + 2 = 35$.
Summarize Ideas	What have you learned about surface area?
Describe or Define	What is a tessellation?
Compare and Contrast	How are trapezoids and parallelograms alike? How are they different?
Reflect on Learning	What was easy about today's lesson? What was hard?

Selecting writing tasks that promote specific types of student thinking will help you make the most of writing in your math classroom. Let's explore the benefits of each type of writing and discuss practical ideas for supporting students as they write. On the CD you will find a variety of customizable writing tasks correlated to sixth- through eighth-grade math content standards.

Explain a Process

Asking students to explain a procedure is a frequently posed math writing task. And that makes perfect sense! Math is full of procedures. Students are faced with multi-step computations or problem-solving tasks and need to find a means, a procedure, for getting to the solution. Asking students to explain *how* they got their answer pushes them to think about the steps they took to get there and helps us assess whether those steps were reasonable. The goal in this type of writing is not for students to follow a template, but for them to be able to clearly express how they moved toward a solution. We are not looking for all students to use the same steps; our goal is for students to be able to verbalize the steps they have used.

Practical Ideas for Helping Students Explain a Process

When you have asked your students to explain how they got an answer, have you ever heard remarks like these?

"I did it in my head."
"I used my calculator."

These responses show a misunderstanding of the question. When students are asked to explain how, we are asking for more detail, for steps and order, not for broad general statements.

"I used the data on the table."
"I made an equation to solve it."

These students are, at least, beginning to refer to the math, but their comments are still too general and do not give us enough detail to understand how they got their answer. What data did they use from the table? What did they do with the data to get the answer? What equation helped them to solve the problem? Helping your students understand the question and what you expect in an answer is a key to getting appropriate responses. When you ask your students to tell you how they did something, do they understand your expectations? Do they know that you expect more than broad, general statements and that you want to see details—specific steps—so that you can follow along with their thinking? Students learn this "how to" writing in language arts class, but they often do not transfer their understanding to writing about math. A typical example of this type of writing is recipes. We learn that an effective way to record the steps in a recipe is by using a numbered list like the following:

1. Preheat the oven to 350°.

2. Grease a 13″ by 9″ pan.

3. Blend the cake mix with 1 cup of water and 3 eggs.

4. Pour the mixture into the greased pan.

5. Bake it for 35 minutes.

The reader clearly understands each step of the task and the order in which the steps should be done. But there are other ways to clearly write procedures. In language arts, we might show the recipe written in paragraph form. Certain words appear in that paragraph to support understanding.

First, preheat the oven to 350 degrees. Next, grease a 13″ × 9″ pan. Then, blend the cake mix with 1 cup of water and 3 eggs. Next, pour it into the pan. Finally, bake it for 35 minutes.

Sequence or transition words such as *first, next,* and *then* help to highlight the order and separate the steps. The procedure is still quite clear. Both numbered lists and sequence words provide a structure to support students' writing and ensure that it will be clearly understood. In addition, the use of these writing structures helps students organize their thinking as they write. The numbers or sequence words cue students to think about both the separate steps they used and the order in which they moved through the steps.

In the middle grades, students have already been introduced to these writing skills, but they are likely to need help in making the connection between what they have learned in language arts class and how it might support them as they apply it to math writing. Stopping to suggest or demonstrate the use of a numbered list or posting the sequence words on your classroom wall will remind students of these possibilities for organizing their writing.

Clarify the Task　Because asking students to explain *how* they did something is a procedural question, we want to make sure they understand the task. Equating it to writing directions can help students better understand what they are being asked to do. Directions might be in various formats (e.g., a paragraph or a list), but they always specify steps and order.

Use Graphic Organizers　Help students organize their writing with graphic organizers. Numbered lists help students identify and record their steps, but sequence chains (see Figure 5–2) are also effective tools to help students organize their thinking. Have students create boxes for each step of the procedure or have them record their steps on one of the sequence chain templates on the CD.

Use Sequence Words　Referring to sequence words when students are verbally explaining processes and posting the words on your classroom wall will remind students to use them in their writing. Some frequently used words are

　　First . . . Second . . . Third . . .
　　First . . . Next . . . Then . . . Last . . .
　　To begin with . . . Finally . . . And so . . . I concluded that . . .

Link Explanations to Problem Situations　When explaining solutions to math problems, students often list their computations without linking them to the problem (i.e., "I did 3 × 8.95 and added 3.95 and got 30.80 and multiplied by .15 and got 4.62."). While that may be what was done mathematically, the explanation lacks a connection to the problem, so the reader may not understand what is being explained. Remind students to link the numbers to the problem situation to allow others to understand what was done and why it was done. Helping students to elaborate on their steps by

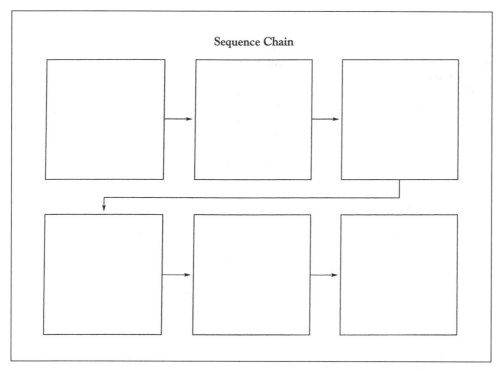

Sequence Chain

Figure 5–2 *Sequence chains allow students to graphically represent the steps in a procedure.*

showing a connection to the problem will provide you with a clearer picture of their understanding. "All 3 people had the lunch special, so I multiplied 3 × $8.95 and added the $3.95 for the dessert they split and I got $30.80. Then I multiplied that total by .15 to find out that the 15% tip was $4.62."

And keep in mind that mathematics is a language of numbers and symbols. Some students might opt to explain the process using mostly representations, with labeling to give us insight about their understanding of each number.

1. 3 (people) × $8.95 (cost of lunch special) = $26.85

2. $26.85 (cost for lunch) + $3.95 (cost for dessert) = $30.80 (cost for all food)

3. $30.80 × .15 (15% tip) = $4.62 (amount of tip)

The labeling, combined with the representations, allows us to follow the student's thinking as she moves toward a solution to the problem.

Show Representations   Encourage students to include representations (numbers and pictures) with their explanations. Showing their work, by including their computations or drawing a diagram, helps to complete their explanation. If the representations are labeled adequately, they can provide us with a great deal of information about students' thinking.

The King Pins

The King family's bowling team, The King Pins, has five members. Their team's mean score in the bowling tournament was 157.

The King Pins
Bowling Scores

Player	Score
Jason	140
Katie	155
Allison	148
Brendan	165
Pat	x

1. What was Pat's score? Explain how you found your answer.

Pat's score was 177. To find the answer I first wrote an equation:

$$157 = \frac{140 + 155 + 148 + 165 + X}{5}$$

Then I solved $(5) \, 157 = \frac{608 + X}{5} (5)$

$$785 = 608 + X$$

$$177 = X$$

Last I checked my work and 157 does equal $\frac{140 + 155 + 148 + 165 + X}{5}$

Figure 5–3 *We are able to clearly follow this student's process for solving the problem.*

We ask students to explain how they got an answer when we want them to identify precisely how they moved toward a solution to a problem (see Figure 5–3). This writing task pushes students to recognize the steps they take in solving math problems and allows us to detect incorrect procedures and to then step in to clarify our students' procedural knowledge.

C L A S S R O O M - T E S T E D   T I P

Recognizing Steps

Some students have difficulty identifying the steps they took to solve a multi-step problem and so have difficulty explaining the procedure. Consider having students solve the problem and then go back to their calculations, placing a (1) by the first thing they did, then a (2) by the next, and so on. Students can then use the number cues to help them write their explanation. As they look at number 1, they simply write what they did in that step, and then continue to number 2. Many students have increased success when they can break down the multi-step task into separate steps before beginning their writing.

Generalize or Draw Conclusions

An important mathematical skill is the ability to analyze data and draw conclusions or generalizations based on the data. Writing tasks are a way to guide students toward discovering mathematical rules or generalizations. Lessons can be crafted to guide students' thinking as they gather, record, and analyze mathematical information. Through creating inquiry-based activities that challenge students to observe, analyze, and generalize, teachers can capitalize on writing as a tool to guide students' thinking and to enable them to record their insights.

Practical Ideas for Writing to Generalize

Recording observations and data is an important part of writing to generalize. As students look back on recorded data, discoveries often occur. Modeling the recording of data, on chart paper or the board, and then using think-aloud techniques to show how we might review and analyze the data helps our students visualize the process going on in our heads.

The Power of Talk   Allow students to work in pairs or groups as they analyze math data and attempt to verbalize rules and generalizations. Have them discuss possible rules or generalizations with their partner or team prior to sharing with the class. Asking them to "Turn and share with a partner" is a great way to ensure that students have discussed their insights prior to whole-class sharing.

Two-Column Notes   Two-column notes are an effective graphic organizer for recording observations and conclusions during manipulative activities or math investigations. Provide students with a worksheet (see the template on the CD) or ask students to fold a paper in half vertically and label one column *Observations* and the other column *Conclusions*. Or you might label the columns *Our Data* and *Our Conclusions*. Students then record their ideas in the appropriate columns.

Investigation	
Observations	Conclusions

Guess My Rule

Function tables are a useful tool for stimulating observations and generalizations. You might construct an in/out table on the blackboard and begin to record a number in the *In* and then *Out* columns following a rule that has not been shared with your students. Students must work with their partners to discover and describe the rule. Challenge them to use algebraic expressions when describing their rules.

In	Out
1	5
2	7
3	9
n	2n +3

Generalizations Through Comparisons   Students might be given lists or examples and then asked to describe their insights based on the examples.

Isosceles Triangles

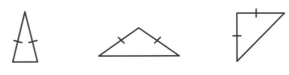

Scalene Triangles

You might ask students what they observe about the triangles based on these examples. Have them jot down observations and discuss them with a partner. Prompt students to share their observations and conclusions. Through observing examples, our students are able to share insights and draw conclusions as they deepen their understanding of triangles.

Justifying an Answer or Process

We ask students to justify their answers when we want to stimulate their reasoning and ensure that their reasoning makes sense. This is the *why* question: "So, you got the answer, but why is that the right answer? Can you defend it with math data? Can you justify it with some type of reasoning? Can you prove that your answer makes sense?" Justifying answers generally requires a *because* statement or an explanation to support the ideas presented. The statements should convince the reader that the answer is correct or the method is appropriate.

Problem: Katie ate 2 slices of pizza. Brendan ate $\frac{1}{2}$ of the pizza. What fraction of the pizza was left?

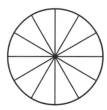

Answer: One-third of the pizza was left.

Answer with justification: One-third of the pizza was left because Brendan ate 1/2 of the pizza which is 6 of the 12 slices, and Katie ate 2 slices, so together they ate 8 of the 12 slices of pizza. Four slices were left, which is 4/12 of the pizza. Then you simplify it to 1/3 of the pizza.

A justification asks students to give data and/or reasoning to prove that their answer is correct. You will have to decide how much detail you want your students to provide and then clearly model your expectations for them. Is this enough?

"There is 1/3 of the pizza left because Brendan ate 6 pieces and Katie ate 2."

Would you like a better understanding of where the student got the fraction to represent the remaining pizza? Perhaps labeling the pizza diagram would help provide the data you need. Using diagrams along with words can strengthen justifications. Do some examples in class to model possibilities for justifying with specific data.

Frequently ask students to justify their solutions orally in class. When they are speaking too generally, ask them for more specific data to prove their point. As they hear each other's justifications, they strengthen their ability to express their ideas and construct clear arguments to support their thinking (see Figure 5–4).

Practical Ideas for Justifying an Answer or Process

Provide lots of opportunities for students to defend their answers and processes in class. You might ask them to turn to a partner and share why they solved a problem in a certain way or why they believe their answer is correct. Have whole-class discussions with students sharing their reasoning. Praise the use of specific data to support answers (see Figure 5–5).

Helpful Words to Clarify the Task   Justifying an answer might be equated to *convincing* someone that your answer is correct. What can you say that will *prove* that the answer makes sense? How can you *defend* your answer? Is there specific data or reasoning that will *support* your answer? Use words like *justify, support, prove, convince,* and *defend* to help students better understand their task.

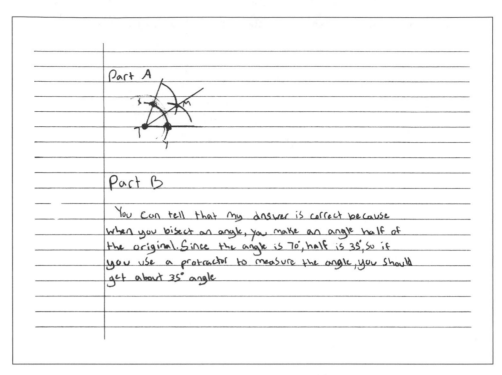

Part A

Part B

You can tell that my answer is correct because
when you bisect an angle, you make an angle half of
the original. Since the angle is 70°, half is 35°, so if
you use a protractor to measure the angle, you should
get about 35° angle

Figure 5–4 *This student constructed a 70° angle and bisected it, then used reasoning and data to defend why his solution must be correct.*

Convince Me!   In this activity, students are asked to provide convincing arguments to support their answers. This can be done orally or in writing and makes a nice warm-up at the start of math class. Students might work with partners to develop their arguments.

■ Convince me: Which is greater: ___ or ___?

Examples:

Which is greater: $3\frac{1}{4}$ feet or $1\frac{1}{6}$ yard?
    Convince me.
    $1\frac{1}{6}$ *yard is greater. To justify, students might convert both measurements to the same unit (i.e., feet or inches), which will allow them to clearly compare the values.*

    Which is the best buy: 5 CDs for $25, 3 CDs for $10, or 10 CDs for $43?
Convince me.
    3 CDs for $10 is the best deal. To justify, students might determine the approximate cost per CD in each situation and then compare the values.

Eliminate It!   The Eliminate It! activity introduced in Chapter 4 to support vocabulary requires students to justify their reasoning as they eliminate one of four words. This activity can also be done by inserting numbers in the four squares on the worksheet (see the template on the CD). Students might be asked to determine which num-

Sharon received $95 for her birthday. She wants to spend her money at The Teen Shop on new clothes and at Bargain Books on books.

- Step A
Write an inequality describing how much money Sharon can spend at each store.
- Step B
Use what you know about inequalities to justify why your inequality is correct. Use words, numbers, and/or symbols in your justification.

Step A

$$x + y \leq 95$$

Step B I know that Sharon recieved $95, and wants to spend it shopping at 2 stores. The money she spends can equal, but not excede, $95. So, $x + y \leq 95$, where x and y are the money she spends at The Teen Shop and Bargain Books, and 95 is the limit. The money Sharon spends at each The Teen Shop and Bargain Books must be less than or equal to $95 when added together.

Figure 5–5 *This student supplies specific math data to justify her answer.*

ber does not belong: 21, 63, 24, 35. Perhaps students eliminate 24 because it is an even number and the others are odd numbers. Or they may eliminate 24 because it is the only one in the set that is not a multiple of 7. Other students might eliminate 35 because it is the only one in which the sum of the digits is not divisible by three. In Eliminate It!, students must analyze words or numbers in a set and then justify their decision as to which one should be eliminated.

Agree or Disagree   In Agree or Disagree, students are given a statement and must either agree or disagree with the statement and then record evidence to support that decision. This activity can be done independently or with a partner. Connecting the statements to the specific math content being studied will provide a perfect opportunity to reinforce content as you coach students to more effectively justify their decisions. The template for Agree or Disagree can be found on the CD.

CLASSROOM-TESTED TIP

The Power of Pictures

Whether a student struggles with written language and must rely on diagrams to communicate or he or she excels at written language and uses diagrams to enhance his/her writing, illustrations are a tremendous support for expressing ideas. For class warm-ups, have students illustrate a word or concept. You might ask them to draw a right triangle or to illustrate complementary and supplementary angles. Ask students to label their pictures with words or phrases. Once students have had some opportunities to communicate their understanding through pictures, remind them of the power of pictures as they write about their math ideas. As students are describing a rotation or reflection, could you suggest that a picture might help convey meaning? The combination of text and pictures/diagrams will become a powerful tool for helping your students communicate about math.

Create Word Problems

Many students perform math operations in a rote fashion but lack understanding of what they are doing. They have memorized the procedure for computing $1.5 \times 4 = x$ but do not understand the connection between the equation and a problem situation that shows $1.5 \times 4 = x$. Writing word problems is a technique that helps students make the connection between equations and problem situations. Students might be asked to write problems to match an equation.

> Equation: $2x + 5 = 11$
>
> Jason and Earl wrote: "We bought 2 ice cream sundaes and split a pizza that cost $5.00. Altogether we paid $11.00. How much did each sundae cost? (x = cost of a sundae; x = $3.00)"

These students demonstrated their understanding of the numbers and symbols in the equation through the writing of their story. We spend a great deal of effort helping our students perform computations. It is equally important that they understand those computations.

Practical Ideas for Creating Word Problems

Asking students to write word problems can be easily linked to computation lessons. If you are teaching students division of decimals, prompt students to write decimal division stories. If you are working on ratios and proportions, ask them to write a word problem to show their understanding of the skill. Combining computational skills and word problems is a healthy way for students to learn the rote skill while developing an understanding of the computation process (see Figure 5–6).

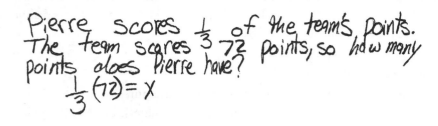

Figure 5–6 *Students write sports word problems to demonstrate their
understanding of equations.*

Talk About It   Allow students to work with groups or partners to design word
problems. Writing word problems can be a difficult task for students who are just developing their understanding of computations. Partner or group support will allow
them to talk about their ideas and develop a story as a team. Once the team has designed a problem, have them record both the problem and the equation to share with
the class.

Reverse It   Present students with a word problem. Ask them to write the equation
that matches the word problem. Have them label what each number in their equation represents.

   Writing word problems helps students make the connection between numbers
and symbols and the situations that those numbers and symbols represent. Along
with writing problems to illustrate equations, students might be asked to write problems that relate to a specific type of computation (e.g., dividing decimals), or problems that can be solved using a certain formula (e.g., $A = L \times W$), or problems that
must be solved using at least two steps. Connect the writing of word problems to the
computational skills you are teaching.

Summarize Ideas

It is extremely beneficial for students to be asked to summarize their ideas. It pushes
them to think about what they have heard or experienced, to identify what they have

learned, and often to recognize what might still be confusing them. Summaries focus on big ideas, not every little detail! In writing about what has been learned about volume, your students might consider these big ideas:

What is volume?

How do we measure the volume of various solid figures?

Why do we need to understand volume? When might it be useful to us?

Rather than explaining every small detail, summaries ask students to identify key ideas about a topic. They are a useful writing task to bring closure to the end of a lesson. They might guide a summation of the week's learning or might be used at the end of a math exploration or unit of study.

Practical Ideas for Summarizing

When writing summaries, students are required to analyze what they have learned and select and record important ideas. This process helps them review previous lessons and remember key ideas. Students sometimes experience difficulty when writing summaries and benefit from lots of modeling and group writing tasks.

KWL KWL charts are tools on which students record (K) what they know about a topic, (W) what they want to learn (or wonder) about the topic, and (L) what they have learned (see the template on the CD). The first two parts of the activity (What I Know and What I Want to Know) are done at the beginning of a unit or topic, while the last part (What I Learned) is done as the unit is progressing or at the end of the unit. The information recorded in the (L) *What I Learned* column provides information that can be used to create a unit summary. For more ideas on using KWL charts, see the first Classroom-Tested Tip in Chapter 7.

Tips List Rather than having students write summary paragraphs, consider asking them to summarize their ideas by creating a Tips List. Ask students to work with a partner or group to come up with their top tips to share with a class who has not yet studied this topic. Students might be asked to make a list of:

Tips for Multiplying and Dividing Decimals

Tips for Determining Surface Area

Tips for Solving Logic Matrix Problems

Graphic Organizers To summarize is to briefly present the main points. When teaching students to summarize, it is important that they can identify the big idea as well as some important supporting points. Graphic organizers can be helpful. Try the organizer in Figure 5–7 or see the additional ideas on the CD including All About. . . , and Sum It Up.

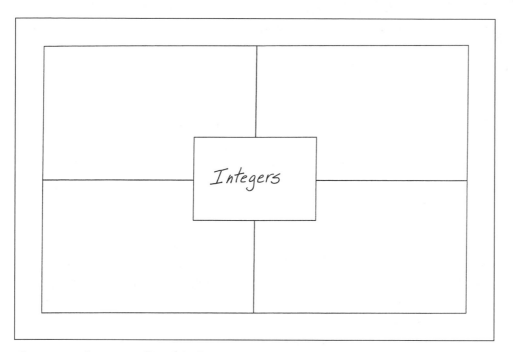

Figure 5–7 *Summary Graphic Organizer*

We know the instructional significance of providing opportunities for closure when ending lessons or units. Writing summaries helps students sum up their ideas and record what they have learned. It helps them make connections between various bits of learning and allows us to assess whether they have acquired key ideas.

Describe or Define

Often, we want to know what students have internalized about a math term or concept. Rather than asking them to select from a multiple-choice list, asking students to describe the term or concept allows us to see what they know. Instead of just selecting from a list and possibly selecting a correct answer even without an understanding of the concept, our students must describe or define a term or concept in their own words, revealing their level of understanding.

Students often have difficulty describing or defining terms. They sometimes answer in short, general statements (e.g., "Polygons are shapes."). This answer does not help us assess their understanding and does not push students to think deeply about the concept. Again, students must be aware of our expectations for their response. We need to make sure that students understand ways to make their definitions specific and clear.

Word choice is a critical element in clear descriptions. Using appropriate vocabulary helps students better communicate their ideas. Illustrations and examples allow students to convey their understandings. Pictures can help clarify the terms. Citing examples (e.g., mentioning that triangles, quadrilaterals, and pentagons are polygons) can help to communicate what they have learned. The goal is for them to get their ideas out of their heads and onto the paper.

Practical Ideas for Writing Definitions and Descriptions

Many students do not know how to write effective descriptions, particularly about math terms and concepts. Helping them recognize ways to express their understanding through words, illustrations, examples, and numbers will provide them with options as they struggle to express their ideas in written form.

Modeling How to Write Clear Definitions   Choose a word and have students work with partners to define the word or describe the concept. Then have two sets of partners share their definitions and together come up with one definition that they consider to be thorough and clear. Have each group of four read their definition to the class. Compile an exemplary definition using the best points from all of the groups. Discuss what made the class definition an exemplary one. Did it include specific vocabulary? Did it include a visual? Did an example help make it clearer? Talk with students about specific ways to make their descriptions clearer.

Folded Books   In Chapter 4 we discussed the value of folded books to help develop math vocabulary (refer back to Figure 4–1). Creating folded books to record descriptions or definitions is a fun way to engage students in descriptive writing. Have students label the front with the word or term and then encourage the use of words, pictures, numbers, and examples to describe the term inside their books.

Word Banks   To encourage students to elaborate on their ideas, consider providing word banks when asking students to describe or define a concept. Rather than simply saying "Describe a square pyramid," to which you might get "A square pyramid is a solid shape," consider asking students to "Describe a square pyramid using the words in the word bank."

Word Bank

faces
edges
vertices

Asking students to define or describe a math concept using words from a word bank pushes students to elaborate on their ideas, to use appropriate vocabulary, and to make connections between math terms.

The goal is not to generate student descriptions or definitions that look like textbook definitions, but rather to help students construct definitions that are clear and complete and allow others to understand the concept that is being described.

A Word about Communicating Through Examples

Examples are powerful ways to express ideas. Asking students to list examples for a math concept is a quick and easy writing task, and the items they place on their lists can effectively demonstrate their understanding of a concept. You might ask students to fold a paper in half and list examples of polygons on one side and polyhedrons on the other side. They might be asked to list times where they might have to calculate percents or list items that have rotational symmetry.

Lists help students see the strength of examples for conveying ideas. The use of examples to bring clarity to students' ideas is an important communication tool. Moving from lists of examples to helping students use examples in their writing will enhance their writing skills.

Compare and Contrast

In order to compare and contrast ideas, students must think about each idea and consider similarities and differences between them. This process of finding commonalities and differences requires students to delve deeper into their understanding of each concept. Students might recognize that a fraction is a part of a whole or a part of a set, but being asked to compare fractions to decimals will force them to think more deeply about the concepts. If both are parts of a whole, then how are they different? Why are they different? In what instances might each be used?

Regardless of the math topic, having students compare and contrast prompts them to talk and write about math ideas. In the student work in Figure 5–8, the student lists the characteristics of a triangular prism and then explains how they differ from the characteristics of a rectangular prism. Asking students to compare and contrast math concepts prompts them to analyze details related to the concepts and stimulates insights about the math ideas.

Practical Ideas for Comparing and Contrasting

In writing comparisons, students benefit from the use of graphic organizers like Venn diagrams (see the template on the CD), to help them record their thoughts in a systematic way. Two-column notes (see the template on the CD) can also provide a helpful way to organize ideas, with students labeling columns *How They Are Alike* and *How They Are Different*.

While Venn diagrams and two-column notes (see Figure 5–9) may be used to organize information to be converted to a paragraph or other writing assignment, they can also be an end product. Students' ideas, recorded on the organizers, are a clear written product to show their understanding.

Instead of finding the surface area of a rectangular prism, we will find the surface area of a triangular prism. Discuss with your partner and make a list of what you know about triangular prisms.

- 5 faces   - 9 edges
- 3 rectangles   - 6 vertices
- 2 triangles

How does a triangular prism differ from a rectangular prism?

A triangular prism has 5 faces and a rectangular prism has 6. A triangular prism has 6 verticies and a rectangular prism has 8 vertices. A triangular prism has 9 edges and a rectangular prism has 12 edges.

Figure 5–8 *This student shares her understanding of the characteristics of triangular prisms, contrasting them to those of rectangular prisms.*

Rectangles and Trapezoids	
How They Are Alike	How They Are Different

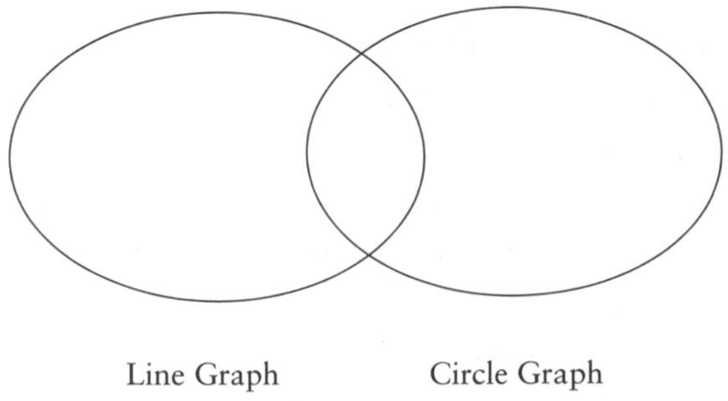

Line Graph   Circle Graph

Figure 5–9 *Tools for recording similarities and differences.*

Choosing the Right Words   If students will be asked to write paragraphs to compare and contrast concepts, consider brainstorming key words for comparing or contrasting. Ask students to generate words they might use when they are indicating that two things are alike and words they might use when they are indicating that two things are different. Some typical words might include:

Words That Compare

both, similar, alike, also, like, same as

Words That Contrast

different, but, however, on the other hand, in contrast

The incorporation of these words will make your students' writing clearer.

CLASSROOM-TESTED TIP

Homework to Preview or Review

Fit some writing into homework tasks to either focus students on the topic for the following day or to provide an opportunity for students to summarize, process, and reflect on the day's teaching.

To Preview

1. Make a list of places, other than school, in which you might see decimals (or any math topic).

2. Read pages 43–46. Write five vocabulary words that will be important in this unit. Record an illustration or example for each one.

3. Read pages 21–23. Make a list of four key ideas to share in class tomorrow.

4. Interview an adult in your family to find out how they use measurement (or any math topic) at work and at home.

To Review

1. Tell me two important things you learned in math class today.

2. What is one thing you know about _____ that you did not know last week? What is one question you have?

3. Write three questions that would be a good quiz for what we did in class today.

4. Compare what we learned about _____ today to what we learned last week.

5. How might you use what you learned in math today?

Reflect on Learning

Reflective writing allows students to express their ideas about mathematics and how they are feeling about learning mathematics. In reflective writing, there is no right or wrong answer; students are simply asked to share their thoughts and ideas. We might ask students to tell us what they know and what might be confusing them or what has been easy or hard about a lesson. Reflective writing provides students with an opportunity to share frustrations, questions, and accomplishments with us (see Figure 5–10). Students may not open up immediately. Sharing frustrations or confusions with their teacher can feel threatening, but once students see that you will respond to their writing by reviewing a concept or answering a question, they will be more likely to share their confusions and frustrations at the next opportunity. It is unlikely that middle grades students will raise their hand and tell you, with the whole class listening, that they don't understand what you have taught, so writing gives them a more private way to alert you to their feelings and confusions.

Writing that encourages student reflection should not be graded; however, your responses to students' reflective writing encourage them to continue to share their thoughts and may offer needed encouragement or support. Many teachers find that their responses to students' reflective writing begin a personal dialogue with certain students. Rather than generic responses like "Great idea!" or "Nice work!" consider responses that clarify students' ideas ("Keep in mind that similar figures do not have to be the same size."), ask additional thought-provoking questions ("Is there another

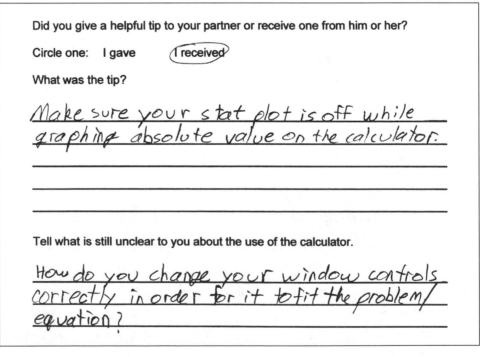

Did you give a helpful tip to your partner or receive one from him or her?

Circle one: I gave   (I received)

What was the tip?

Make sure your stat plot is off while graphing absolute value on the calculator.

Tell what is still unclear to you about the use of the calculator.

How do you change your window controls correctly in order for it to fit the problem/ equation?

Figure 5–10 *This student shares something he has learned about using a calculator and asks a question to clarify his confusion.*

way you could have solved that problem?") or build students' confidence ("You remembered the formula and applied it perfectly!").

Practical Ideas for Reflecting on Learning

Students look forward to your response to their writing. It is best to assign this type of prompt only as frequently as you are able to respond to your students. And reflective writing is time-sensitive. If we ask students to tell us what they are having difficulty with on a Tuesday, it is important that we review their writing immediately. Finding out a week later that most of the class was struggling with a concept last Tuesday is no help to our students. Here are some tips for making the task doable.

Two-Column Notes   The two-column note format (refer to the template on the CD) is very versatile, as the teacher simply fills in the headings to direct student work. Two-column notes might be used for reflective writing with the following headings:

> I Understand/My Questions
> This Was Easy/This Was Hard
> I Know This/I Am Confused About This
> I Could Teach This/I Need to Hear This Again
> Skills I Know/Skills I Need to Practice

Quick Reflections   For quick reflections, give each student a blank index card at the end of math class. Ask students to label the sides of their card with the numbers 1 and 2. Pose a reflective prompt for each side (e.g., "On side 1 write a fact you learned and on side 2 write a question you have"). Because of the limited space on the cards, students will need to get to the point and you will be able to quickly review how they are doing.

Sentence Starters   Sentence starters are great ways to stimulate reflections. Ask students to finish one of these lines:

> I think it's easy to . . . I think it's hard to . . .
> I'm glad I can . . . I wish I could . . .
> During math class, I felt . . .
> Today I made this mistake . . . I learned . . .
> When I get stuck on a math problem, I . . .

Post It   Provide students with sticky notes and designate a place for them to post their questions or insights about the lessons (see Figure 5–11). The insights and questions might be shared at the start of the next class to summarize important ideas and clarify misunderstandings.

Figure 5–11 *Students might use sticky notes to post their questions following a lesson.*

Reading students' reflective writing provides us with tremendous insights. We learn who might be feeling insecure, bored, or overwhelmed. Our students' reflections help us identify skills that may need to be retaught, and they remind us that students do not always learn at the pace in which we teach.

Math Journals

Math journals are generally thought of as bound books in which students record various math writing tasks. Math journals provide a spot for students to do the following things:

- brainstorm ideas
- record predictions, observations, and conclusions about math explorations
- list questions
- solve and reflect on math problems

- describe concepts

- justify answers

- explain procedures

- summarize the main points of a lesson

- make connections between math ideas and other content learning

- reflect on learning mathematics

While bound books do have some advantages in that pages cannot be lost and students, as well as teachers and parents, are able to see progress throughout the course of the year, there is no hard and fast rule as to where students should do their math writing. Some teachers prefer to have students write on loose-leaf paper that is placed in a separate binder section. And many teachers find that having students record only selected writing tasks in a journal provides them with certain samples to assess students' progress over time, while still allowing students to engage in some writing tasks outside their journals to sustain their enthusiasm through diverse writing tasks. Students often respond positively to the novelty of writing on chart paper, graph paper, folded paper, transparencies for overhead projectors, green paper, blue paper, or yellow paper—anything that keeps them excited about writing!

CLASSROOM-TESTED TIP

Finding the Time to Write

We have so much to teach and so little time! How can we find the time to add writing into our day? Think about how you are currently using your class time and experiment with some readjustments.

- Incorporate a writing task into your lesson warm-up or as a brief closure activity at the end of your lesson.

- Teaching math computations is critical, but can you modify class assignments to also include some writing/thinking tasks? Perhaps rather than assigning fifteen math computations, you might assign eight computations and one related writing task. Students might be asked to explain how they solved one of the problems, justify an answer, or write a word problem related to one of the computations.

- Modifying homework in the same way (assigning a few less computations to make time for some writing) provides students with opportunities to write about their thinking while providing you with an opportunity to talk about students' math thinking when you are reviewing homework with the class.

- Keep your outcomes in mind and incorporate math writing when it helps you reach those outcomes.

Writing as an Essential Tool for Developing Math Understanding

Just as our verbal questioning is a critical tool to stimulate varied levels of student thinking, balancing the writing prompts that we pose to students allows us to inspire a wide range of thought. When we want students to think about procedures, we ask them to write about how they solved a problem. When we want our students to recognize key learning, we ask them to summarize. When our objective is to strengthen their understanding of equations and their connection to problem situations, we ask them to write word problems. When we want them to delve more deeply into their understanding of concepts, we ask them to compare and contrast concepts. When our objective is to push students' reasoning, we ask them to justify or defend their answers. The writing tasks that we pose should correspond to the thinking we aim to develop. Writing prompts provide us with a myriad of options for stimulating students' thinking.

Students write to learn mathematics, but students must also learn to write *about* mathematics. The complexity of the content, the difficulty of the vocabulary, and the challenges of written language all combine to make writing in math frustrating for many of our students. While supporting and developing their math understandings, we can continue to remind them of ways to clarify their ideas, add details to create thorough writing, and organize their math thinking to allow others to make sense of it. In the following chapter, we explore additional ways to support our students as they work to strengthen their abilities to write about mathematics.

Questions for Discussion

1. What is the role of writing in the math classroom? How does writing about mathematics benefit students? How does it benefit teachers?

2. How can we help students learn to write more effectively about mathematics?

3. What is the role of illustrations, examples, and numeric representations when writing about math?

4. How can an understanding of various types of writing help us select writing tasks that reflect our content objectives?

CHAPTER 6

Supporting Students as They Write

The process of learning to write mathematically is similar to that of learning to write in any genre. Practice, with guidance, is important.

— National Council of Teachers of Mathematics,
Principles and Standards for School Mathematics

Our students need support to be able to write effectively about mathematics. Some will need support in finding words to express their ideas. Others will need help in putting their words into writing. Still others will require assistance clarifying and understanding the math ideas about which they are being asked to write. Our guidance, as they work to develop their skills, is essential.

Supporting Students Through Math Talk

Supporting students as they write about math requires attention to both their math understanding (content skills) and their communication (process skills). Ironically, it is through communication that we can help students develop both content and process skills at the same time. We have discussed the importance of talk in the math classroom. As we talk to students about our math ideas, we are modeling both math thinking and effective ways to communicate that thinking. As students listen to each other in class discussions or small-group activities, they are not only hearing the math ideas, but also hearing the ways their peers express those ideas. Our questions and comments during class discussions can help students further develop their skills.

For example, Mr. Newell asked his students to explain how they solved the proportion $\frac{4}{5} = \frac{x}{20}$. As he listened to their explanations, he was able to provide feedback on both their math ideas and their ability to effectively share those ideas.

"I like the way you explained your thinking, Marty. Telling me each step you took to find the value of x helped me really understand how you did it." (Note the attention to language process.)

"Why did you begin by dividing 20 by 5?" (Note the focus on math thinking.)

When we are attentive to what students say as well as how they say it, we can help them develop math and communication skills simultaneously.

Scaffolding Support

Writing about math is not easy! Even good writers have difficulty transferring their language arts skills to complex math writing. Helping students understand writing about math and supporting them as they develop their skills is critical. Our goal is to find just the right amount of support. We want to guide students as they develop their skills, but allow for increasing independence so students can test their skills. Supporting students is a process of scaffolding the level of support. Consider the following three levels of support:

1. Write Aloud

2. Write Along

3. Write Alone

Write Aloud

This stage provides the greatest support. In this stage, you are doing the writing. Students may need to hear your thinking about a math concept through a think-aloud technique and watch as you write about your ideas. Use chart paper, the blackboard, overhead projector, or video visualizer to model how you would write a response. Talk as you write, or try an interactive approach in which you involve students in brainstorming ideas that you will record. The write-aloud level of support allows students to see and hear the writing process at work. Students of all ages benefit from seeing someone compose and write a response.

Write Along

In this level, students are writing with support. You might ask guiding questions, encourage, and make suggestions as they write, or students may be supported by writing with a group or a partner. Working with peers helps students develop their math ideas, build their math vocabularies, and receive assistance with the writing process.

Write Alone

In this level, students write independently without teacher or peer support. Whether it is an instructional or an assessment task, students' writing reflects their own abilities at that point in time.

Differentiating Support

Seeing demonstrations of math writing, having opportunities for guided writing, and being tested with opportunities to write alone are all steps in learning to write effectively about math. Supporting our students through write-aloud, write-along, and write-alone experiences will provide scaffolded support as students hone their skills. As different types of writing tasks are posed or as the math content gets complex, we may need to readjust the level of support for our students. Students may feel confident to *write alone* for one math topic or writing task but may be at a *write-along* level for another, needing our guidance to move through the task. Determining which level of support is appropriate for various students allows us to differentiate our support to meet their needs (see Figure 6–1).

The level of support we provide does not depend on students' math abilities alone. Gifted students may benefit from a write-aloud as they become frustrated trying to verbalize a math process. While they may be confident that their answer is correct, they may need support explaining how they got that answer. A write-aloud may help them develop the communication skills to express their ideas. Other students may benefit from write-alouds because of their math and communication difficulties. Focusing attention on both the math content and the communication tips during write-alouds will benefit a greater number of students.

Figure 6–1 *Providing students with individual support is essential to their development as writers.*

Clarifying Expectations

Students need to understand our expectations when we ask them to write about math. In Chapter 5, we discussed many types of writing tasks. We mentioned the importance of students understanding the question or task in order to effectively address it. Writing about how you solved a problem is different from describing a concept, justifying an answer, or summarizing key ideas. Clarifying our expectations will help students better meet them. Prior to writing tasks, take time to review your expectations. Cue students to the kind of writing you expect. Are you looking for the steps they took to solve the problem? Do you expect details to support their answers?

We discuss the use of rubrics as an assessment tool in Chapter 8, but rubrics are also an effective previewing tool as they allow our students to better understand our expectations and pinpoint what we will be looking for in their writing. By reviewing rubrics with our students prior to a writing task, we are able to verbalize our expectations for both the content and communication aspects of their writing.

And while setting expectations should happen prior to a writing task, clarifying expectations can happen throughout or even after a task is completed. Through clear and specific feedback, we can continue to show our students how to strengthen their math writing. Our students should know what will make us smile and what is likely to disappoint us when we see a piece of writing. Providing students with specific feedback will help them understand our expectations, but what are some effective ways to provide feedback to students?

Feedback to Improve Writing

Students need ongoing feedback to improve their writing about math. The feedback process is intended to take what students have done and help them analyze it, reflect on it, and improve it. Rather than a feed*back* process, it may be more accurate to think of it as a feed *forward* process as the goal is for students to internalize the feedback to improve future work. As our students write, it is critical that we continually provide them with feedback on both their ideas and their communication of those ideas. And it is important they continue to reflect on both.

In order to be helpful, feedback must be frequent and specific. Frequently providing tips for improving work, commenting on students' progress, and helping students analyze and improve their writing allows them to tackle it in small steps. And specific feedback allows them to see exactly how to improve their work. Rather than simply showing an exemplary piece of writing, consider sharing specifically why the writing is effective. Did the student select vocabulary words that made his ideas clear? Did the student provide data or reasoning to justify his math ideas? Did including a labeled diagram help make the math idea understandable? Highlighting the specifics will help your students know how to better communicate their own math ideas.

Written feedback is certainly important. Scoring students' writing and providing them with opportunities to look at your comments and ratings will help many students better understand how to improve their work. But not all students understand our comments on their papers, or even read our comments, so finding the time to discuss feedback with the whole class is important.

Mr. Bright frequently conducts class critiques with his seventh graders following writing assignments. He selects a student paper that has good qualities but can be improved, or he creates a writing sample with some good qualities and room for improvement, and then displays the writing on the overhead projector. When using real student work, he never shows, or says, the student's name and does not use any work that would embarrass a student. After putting the work sample on the overhead, he asks students to read it and work with a partner to identify its good qualities and to find ways to make it even better (see Good, Better Best template on the CD). Guiding questions include the following:

1. What is good about this math response?

2. What could we do to make it even better?

Partners share their ideas with the class. Mr. Bright has students engaged in finding specific ways to improve their understanding of math ideas (content) and communication about those ideas (process).

Finding ways to focus students on analyzing their own work, and ultimately improving their work, is critical. Through reviewing rubrics and expectations, providing frequent and specific feedback, conducting class critiques, and facilitating guided rewrites (see the Classroom-Tested Tip below), we help students understand ways to improve their writing about math.

CLASSROOM-TESTED TIP

Guided Rewrites

For students to improve their writing, it is essential that they understand the qualities of good writing. Facilitating guided rewrites is one way to focus them on ways to improve their work. A guided rewrite consists of the following steps:

1. Students are asked to independently write about a topic (e.g., *Explain how to create a stem-and-leaf plot.*).

2. After students have finished their writing, the teacher asks them to turn their papers over (so they are unable to continue writing) and facilitates a discussion about reasonable responses to the prompt in order to stimulate ideas for improving their writing. The teacher might ask:

   ■ What key vocabulary might I hear when someone is explaining this type of graph?

   ■ Would an example help someone understand how to create it?

   ■ Would a diagram make it clearer?

   ■ What would you do first? Next?

- Would someone understand how to create a stem-and-leaf plot after reading your explanation?

3. Students are then asked to write an improved response. The goal is not to include all of the ideas presented, but to select something that they feel improves their response.

4. The teacher asks students to talk about or write about how they improved their work.

Guided rewrites provide students with opportunities to reflect on ways to improve their own writing.

Support for Struggling Students

Some students have more difficulty writing about math than others. While all students benefit from varied levels of support (e.g., write aloud, write along, write alone), frequent and specific feedback, partner and group discussions to clarify their ideas, and vocabulary development to help them find words to express their ideas, some students may require additional interventions to develop their skills.

We recognize that these instructional interventions may not be permitted during our accountability testing programs; however, we also recognize the inherent difference between assessment and instruction. While assessment is intended to determine what students can do, often without support, instruction is a process of supporting students as they learn. Through our interventions we are able to help students improve their skills. As their skills develop, we remove some supports and provide them with more opportunities to show what they know independent of our help. Our goal is for our students to develop skills during instruction so they will be able to demonstrate those skills at assessment time. Following are some ideas for supporting your struggling students before, during, and after writing tasks.

Before Writing: Understanding the Question or Task

- Many students have difficulty reading the question or prompt. Read the question aloud to students or have them read it with a partner.

- If there is challenging vocabulary in the question, discuss the words and their meanings.

- After reading the question, have the class generate a list of related vocabulary words.

- Allow students to brainstorm with a partner prior to beginning the task in order to generate some ideas about the content.

■ Begin the assignment with the students. You might compose the first part with them to get them focused prior to having them write independently.

■ Remind students to use math vocabulary logs, dictionaries, or word walls to assist them in selecting words to use in their written responses.

■ If students are having difficulty getting started, ask them to jot down ideas, draw a picture, or write with a free-flow technique to get the ideas flowing.

■ Provide sentence starters or cloze techniques (blanks within a sentence) to jump-start student writing. (e.g., "I solved this problem by . . ." or "There are ___ chairs in the auditorium. I found my answer by . . . I know this answer is correct because. . . .")

■ Try some cooperative learning strategies to get students talking about their thinking. In read-talk-solve, students read the problem with a partner, talk about how they might solve it, and then solve it independently.

■ Use think-alouds to share your own thinking about a similar problem (e.g., "Well, first I thought I'd. . . , but then I noticed . . . so I decided to . . .").

■ Have students use graphic organizers to list and organize their thoughts prior to writing.

During Writing

■ Circulate through the room during writing tasks to monitor student progress. Based on your observations, pull a small group to do a think-aloud while others work alone or prompt individual struggling students with supporting questions.

■ Have class "time-outs" to share ideas to get students unstuck. Ask for "tips" from the class to jump-start those who might be struggling.

■ For multi-step problems or tasks, have students cross off directions as they complete them.

■ Encourage students to ask for help. You might assign partners so students can ask a classmate for help, or you might have a signal for students to get your attention when they need help (e.g., raising their index finger).

After Writing

■ After assignments are completed, discuss possible responses.

■ Allow students to revise and rewrite their assignments when appropriate.

■ Facilitate peer reviews to provide students with feedback to improve their work.

■ Invite struggling students to talk with you about their writing. Have them explain their work. Offer tips to support them.

Modifying the Writing Task

■ Allow additional time for students to complete the writing task (i.e., allow students to complete work at home or allow them to have ten extra minutes in class).

■ Give a shorter writing assignment (i.e., ask students to make a list of five items instead of ten items, or write one paragraph instead of two paragraphs).

■ Consider tasks that require less writing and may be completed with lists, labeled diagrams, or examples.

Adaptations for Students with Special Needs

Some students have specific disabilities that are recorded on their Individual Education Plans (IEPs). These students may require modifications when they are writing about math. Consider some of the following:

Quantity

Modify the number of items that the student is expected to complete.

Time

Modify the time allowed for the task.

Level of Support

Increase the amount of assistance given (i.e., provide personal conferences to look over the student's work, or assign a peer buddy for support).

Input

Modify the instructional delivery (i.e., allow the student to work with a partner, or provide sentence starters).

Difficulty Level

Modify the skill level (i.e., simplify the task directions or assign questions with a different level of difficulty).

Output

Modify how the student shows understanding (i.e., instead of requiring the student to answer a problem in writing, allow the student to respond verbally or using a word processor, or allow the student to list items rather than write complete paragraphs).

Participation

Modify the student's level of involvement in the task (i.e., assign a group recorder so the student can simply add her ideas to the discussion.)

CLASSROOM-TESTED TIP

As Easy as 1, 2, 3

We often ask students to explain how they got an answer, but many have difficulty identifying the steps they took or verbalizing their actions. Show students that it's *As Easy as 1, 2, 3*. On the blackboard or overhead, create a chart as shown on the CD. On one side you will be solving a math problem (showing your work); on the other side you will be writing how you solved the problem, step-by-step, numbering the steps 1, 2, 3, and so on. Select a multi-step problem from your textbook or curriculum. Read the problem to your students, then begin solving it on the left side of your chart. Talk to the class as you solve it, possibly asking your students for ideas on what to do next. Stop after each step to write a sentence or phrase on the right side of the chart to verbalize what was just done. Continue until you have solved the whole problem and recorded each step you took. Reread the steps you recorded in the right column. Do they explain how you solved the problem? Modeling this process with your students helps them see how you identify and verbalize your steps in solving the problem, and provides an example of both showing your work (representations) and explaining your work (words). Even good writers and good problem solvers gain insights when watching you model the process.

Parent Support

Parents may feel comfortable helping their children with calculations, but may struggle with reasoning and communication in math. And because they may not have written in math class, they may not understand the critical role of writing. Negative parent comments about writing in math class can often thwart our classroom efforts. Find ways to show the parents of your students that writing about math can benefit their children's understanding of math. Share your ideas with them at your Back-to-School Night. Talk to your principal about having a parent math night at your school. Share ideas in a parent letter or school newsletter (see the Parent Letter on the CD). Help the parents of your students understand how writing and talking about math ideas will help their children. With your guidance, they will be better able to support their children at home.

Creating Positive Attitudes About Math Writing

Writing about math can be a frustrating experience. Provide lots of encouragement. Students who struggle with writing need to be convinced that they can do this. Put away your red pen. Focus on the math ideas that your students are trying to convey, and praise them for finding ways (e.g., pictures, lists, labels, representations) for getting those ideas out of their heads. First allow students to get their ideas in writing and then, with encouragement, help them improve on their ideas.

A combination of student practice and teacher guidance is needed to develop effective writers of mathematics. It is problematic when students dislike writing and do not want to practice writing. It is important that we motivate students with engaging tasks, perhaps having them record ideas from a hands-on activity or explain the process for solving a class investigation. Allowing students to write on construction paper, chart paper. graph paper, or colored paper will spark their interest. Folding paper to create books (see Figure 6–2) or recording ideas on overhead

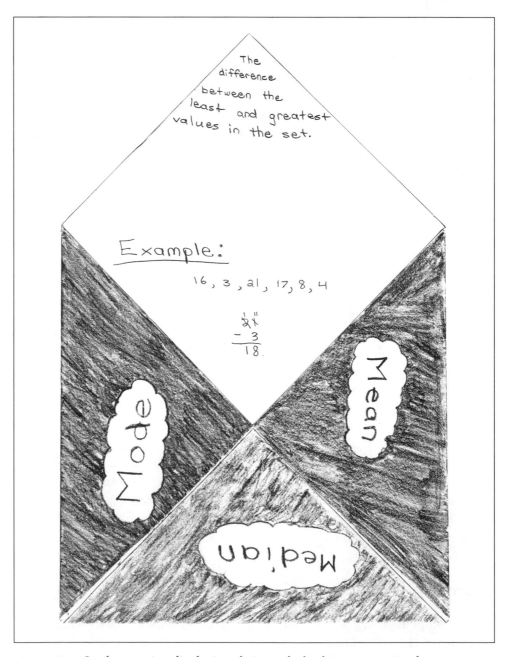

Figure 6–2 *Students enjoy displaying their math thinking in creative formats.*

transparencies for class presentations will generate interest. Praising students for their efforts, encouraging them to improve their skills, and building their confidence in their writing abilities are all critical to the process. And helping students view writing as an essential tool for exploring mathematics, one that is a natural part of math lessons, will help create positive attitudes about writing in math class.

CLASSROOM-TESTED TIP

Peer Review

Peer reviews provide students with opportunities to view others' writing and can result in helpful suggestions; however, students often have difficulty verbalizing effective feedback. Hearing that your writing was "good" does not challenge the reviewer or provide useful information to the writer. Guiding peer reviews with specific questions can lead to more helpful feedback. Choose questions appropriate to the writing task. Some possibilities include:

- Does the description contain enough detail? What additional information might be helpful?

- Is there enough data to support the writer's decision/answer?

- Is the sequence logical, and can it be easily followed?

- Does the writer use appropriate math vocabulary?

- Do you have any questions to ask the writer?

- Is there anything that confuses you about this writing?

Questions for Discussion

1. How might we scaffold support for our students so we can help them develop into independent writers?

2. In what ways can we support students who struggle with writing about math?

3. How might parent attitudes affect student attitudes about writing in math class? How can we create positive attitudes for both parents and students?

CHAPTER 7

Reading About Math

During subject matter study outstanding teachers utilize reading and writing as tools to improve their students' learning of both subject matter and subject-specific literacy strategies.

—Moore, Moore, Cunningham, and Cunningham,
Developing Readers and Writers in the Content Areas K–12

In the past, math tasks were about numbers and computations, so students' reading levels did not significantly affect their performance in math class, but with our increasing focus on math reasoning and problem solving, we are noticing more situations in which students' reading difficulties are impairing their ability to complete math tasks. Reading is a critical way to receive information, and students who experience reading difficulties are often uncertain about problem scenarios, confused about task directions, or unable to gather important information from text. Reading ability influences student achievement across content areas. Whether students are learning science, social studies, or math content, their ability to read the text and the assigned activities determines their ability to understand and perform the tasks. Because we recognize the critical role of reading in acquiring content information or understanding problems or questions, we have seen a major increase in attention to the skills involved in content reading. In this chapter we will explore practical ways to help students read math text. By focusing on critical content reading strategies, we can build our students' reading skills so they can continue to develop their math understandings.

Reading Content Text

Our math books are examples of expository (content) text. While our school reading programs are including more and more expository text selections, our students still have greater exposure to narrative text (e.g., stories, novels). Our students are familiar with identifying the setting and characters of a story or the series of events in narrative text. They are used to the problem-and-resolution format of narrative stories. Expository text has a quite different structure. Rather than characters and settings and events, it is characterized by concepts and definitions and diagrams. Rather than sentences that slowly build a story idea, content text can be saturated with complex ideas and challenging vocabulary. Rather than keeping you on the edge of your seat with suspense as the story unfolds, content text contains a seemingly overwhelming amount of facts and figures. It is easy to understand why students in grades 6 through 8 might struggle with reading math text. Their prior reading experiences may not have prepared them for the complexity of the text, and the content may not intrigue them in the same way that they are intrigued by stories. But developing content reading skills is an important goal for our students. Providing specific lessons focusing on the features of expository text is an important component of intermediate-level reading instruction, but helping students in the middle grades apply their content reading skills as they read their math textbook or their math assignments is also a critical component of their learning experience. During math class, we can and should support our students as they practice making sense of math text.

What Is Reading?

Reading is not simply calling out words. It is a process of getting meaning from those words. A good reader blends his prior knowledge with the words on the page to make sense of the information and acquire new knowledge. Good readers make connections between what they know and the words they read. They visualize ideas, make inferences when ideas are not written in the text, continually question to make sense of ideas, and monitor their own comprehension to be sure they are understanding what they are reading. Being a strategic reader means doing all of those things. We can support students by modeling strategies, prompting them with questions, and providing suggestions and encouragement. Teachers of reading do not have to be reading teachers. Math teachers are equally able to support and guide students as they work to gain more skills at reading math text.

Before-, During-, and After-Reading Strategies

Reading is about making sense of words, and comprehending what we read can be challenging when the concepts get complicated. And math certainly presents some complex concepts! Helping students identify strategies to use before they read, during reading, and after they read will assist them in making sense of the content. Following are some before, during, and after reading strategies that support students in comprehending content text.

Before Reading

Content text contains numerous concepts, lots of specialized vocabulary, and a unique format that can contribute to the difficulty of understanding the text. To process the ideas and understand the words, students must be ready for reading. Simply assigning page numbers for independent reading may not adequately prepare those students who are challenged by the complexities of this type of text. Following are some prereading strategies that will help your students get ready to read.

Access and Develop Prior Knowledge

Since reading is a process of connecting new ideas to existing ones, it is important that students have some prior knowledge about the topic before they begin their reading. If your sixth graders will be reading about proportions, for example, it is important that they first know what a ratio is. Reviewing key ideas prior to reading is essential. Reviewing ideas can be short and informal. You might simply pose a quick "turn and share" during which students tell their partners what a ratio is and then you facilitate a quick class sharing. The new ideas in the text will be better absorbed if your students have background knowledge on which to attach the new ideas.

Preview the Material

Before reading, it is helpful to have students preview the material so they have an idea of what they will be reading about. Prior to reading, you might ask students to skim the pages, looking at pictures, captions, headings, and bold print. Students are not asked to read every word, but just skim the pages to predict the information they will be learning on those pages or to find main ideas. Students might be asked to develop questions that they would like answered in that section of the text. (See the KWL strategy in the Classroom-Tested Tip below.)

CLASSROOM-TESTED TIP

KWL

KWL is a great technique for both previewing information and summarizing information. The technique can be done as a whole-group activity with the teacher recording the class information or as a partner or individual activity with students recording their information. KWL is a three-part activity in which students brainstorm K (What I Know About the Topic), W (What I Want to Know or What I Wonder About the Topic), and L (What I Learned About the Topic).

The first two parts of the activity (What I Know and What I Want to Know) are done at the beginning of a unit or topic, while the last part (What I Learned) is done as the unit is progressing or at the end of the unit. In What I Know (K) students are being asked to access and share prior knowledge about the topic.

The teacher might ask, "What do you already know about analyzing graphs?" and then record students' ideas. The W (What I Want to Know or What I Wonder) can be problematic in mathematics, as students often do not know what they do not know! During this step, students can be asked to skim the chapter, reading headings, diagrams, captions, or bold or italicized print to get an idea of what might be new about the topic. After skimming the chapter, students can more easily generate questions because they recognize words that are unfamiliar to them or skills that they do not know.

- "What are measures of central tendency?"

- "How do you figure out which graph is best to use?"

These questions focus students on new topics and guide their thinking as they move through the unit. In the final part of KWL, the L, students summarize what they have learned and try to answer the questions they generated. Recording KWLs on chart paper that is displayed in the classroom throughout the unit allows students to refer back to their questions. If students are recording their own ideas on a KWL, they might place them in a notebook for reference throughout the unit. KWLs provide a preview and review strategy, along with support for key unit vocabulary.

Create Semantic Maps

Semantic maps (e.g., concept webs) are a great way to focus students on a topic and on key vocabulary related to the topic. Prior to reading about polyhedrons, for example, you might begin a web with the word *solid figures*. Students might be asked to talk to a partner or group and brainstorm related words. You might record some of the words or ideas on the web (e.g., *three-dimensional*, *sphere*, *rectangular prism*, *triangular pyramid*, *edges*, *faces*, *vertices*). The class might discuss the placement of words on their web, placing words in clusters based on their meanings.

"How are faces, edges, and vertices alike and different?"
"Do all of the space figures on our web have edges and vertices?"
"How is a sphere different from a rectangular prism or a triangular pyramid?"

The discussions and recording of these ideas is paving the way for the concept of *polyhedrons* (solid figures that have polygons as sides) and is also reviewing key vocabulary that will certainly affect students' ability to read and understand the text.

Develop Vocabulary

Students need to be able to read the words in order to make sense of the text. Vocabulary development is an important prereading strategy. Previewing the text for vocabulary that might present a challenge to students, and then presenting that vocabulary prior to having them read the text, will support your students in being able to read it more fluently. A variety of vocabulary activities are presented in Chapter 4. These activities can be short, informal, and interactive, such as riddles, word boxes, or quick reviews of word meanings (i.e., "What does this word mean?" "Can someone give me an example?" "Can you use it in a sentence for me?").

Set a Purpose for Reading

Students who will be reading on their own benefit greatly from having a purpose for reading. You might ask students to read to find the answer to a question or to find out more about a topic. Let them know why they will be reading this section of text.

> "We know how to find the surface area of a prism. We are going to read to find out how to find the surface area of a cylinder."
>
> "We are going to read page 237 to find out why it is important to pay attention to whether the coordinates are negative or positive when plotting points on a coordinate plane."

Use Anticipation Guides

Anticipation guides are an engaging technique for getting students to think about topics prior to reading. An anticipation guide is a list of statements about the topic. Students are asked to agree or disagree with each statement (without really knowing the answer—just anticipating what it might be) and then are allowed to look for the material in their text to verify their predictions. Students then read and record whether each statement was correct.

> *Sample Anticipation Guide*
>
> Before you read, put an *A* for agree or a *D* for disagree in the *before* column for each statement. After you read, go back and read each statement again. Put an *A* for agree or a *D* for disagree in the *after* column.

Before		After
_____	1. A trapezoid is a quadrilateral.	_____
_____	2. A square is a rhombus.	_____
_____	3. A rectangle is a parallelogram.	_____

Anticipation guides highlight key ideas. Although students may not know the ideas prior to their reading, they recognize them as they read and become more aware of the content.

During Reading

During the reading process, good readers continually monitor their comprehension of the material. We think about what we are reading. We process the ideas and connect them to previous ideas. Students often need support with the skill of monitoring their own comprehension. Students might be reminded to pay attention to the headings or bold print since these features focus them on the concepts. If material is consumable (e.g., workbooks, worksheets, or copies from a text), having students highlight or underline as they read can help many students focus on the key points. Teachers might model note-taking, recording key ideas after reading sections of the text. Below are some ways to help students focus on the content during the reading process:

- Remind students to pay attention to the headings and bold print, since they are used to emphasize key ideas.

- Cue them to look at the tables and diagrams, since they include lots of content information.

- Tell students to pause now and then and ask themselves "Do I get it?"

- Show them how you stop periodically and summarize what you read.

- Model stopping periodically to jot down key ideas.

Along with helping students identify ways to monitor their own comprehension during the reading process, teachers can support students by asking questions periodically as students are engaged in reading content text. You might ask students to restate a fact or relate an idea to past learning. The questions asked during reading should be short and purposeful so they support students in comprehending the text without distracting them from the content.

After Reading

After reading content text, students benefit from reflecting on the content and summarizing the ideas. Involving students in class discussions about the content helps them process the ideas. Asking comprehension questions or asking students to restate ideas can guide students as they reflect on the content they have read. Students might be asked to reread to find answers to questions.

"Who can read the definition of theoretical probability?"
"What are permutations?"
"How would you find the surface area of a cylinder?"

Asking students to work with partners to design questions about the content is a good way to get them thinking about the important ideas.

Writing summaries is an effective way to help students identify key ideas. You might model writing a summary of the information with students, asking for their ideas and constructing a summary paragraph together, or you might ask students to work with a partner to write a summary of ideas learned in their reading.

Techniques like SQ3R, in which students move through five steps as they survey, question, read, recite, and review information can be helpful for older students as a study technique for reviewing material, as well as a technique to help them construct meaning while reading. In SQ3R, students are challenged to use questions, predict content, set a purpose for reading, and monitor their reading for confusion. SQ3R includes the following steps:

1. *Survey* the headings and think about what you know or want to know about each topic.

2. *Question*: Turn each heading into a question that might be answered as you read that section.

3. *Read* to search for answers to your questions.

4. *Recite*: Test yourself by trying to recall the answers to your questions.

5. *Review* your answers and summarize the information.

Features of Content Text

Reading content text is challenging for students. Each sentence or paragraph is filled with ideas. Content text contains specialized and technical vocabulary that can make it difficult to understand. And the format of the writing, with headings and bold print and diagrams, provides unique challenges if students are unfamiliar with these features. But helping students understand the features of expository text helps unlock the mystery and provides students with the ability to use the text to full advantage.

Recognizing the features of expository text helps our students better locate information and better understand the content. Think-aloud techniques are an effective way to highlight the features of the text and show how you use them to make sense of ideas (i.e., "Oh, that diagram shows a rotation. Now I see what they mean." or "I'm not sure I understand that. I think I'll look that word up in the glossary."). Taking the time to acquaint students with these features will help them better comprehend the content within their math books.

Appendix

The appendix contains additional resources. Typical appendix items in math texts include measurement charts, practice problems, or test preparation materials. While these materials vary from text to text, knowing what is included in your appendix may provide access to helpful resources.

Bold Print or Italics

Bold print or the use of italics is meant to highlight specific words or phrases. Often key vocabulary is bold or italicized so students are able to identify it more easily. The bold or italicized print signals students to pay special attention and to seek out the meaning of those words or phrases.

Diagrams and Labels

Diagrams are graphics that illustrate ideas. Diagrams might include numbers, graphs, tables, or other representations. Diagrams often include labels to identify parts of the diagram (i.e., an arrow to show the height, width, and depth of a rectangular prism). Math textbooks often include diagrams of manipulatives to show concepts (i.e., algebra tiles on a scale to show the process of balancing equations).

Glossary

The glossary provides quick definitions for important words in the text. Because there are so many math vocabulary words, this feature can be very helpful for students. The glossary is located in the back of the book, and entries are organized alphabetically to help students quickly locate definitions. Math glossaries often include illustrations to more effectively define some words.

Headings

Headings are brief phrases that provide a quick preview of the topic in the following section of text. Headings allow the reader to scan and locate the part of the text that addresses a specific topic. Headings might describe general topics (i.e., Integers and the Number Line, Adding Integers) or may help separate textbook sections and identify each section (i.e., Practice, Mixed Review, Problem Solving, Write About It).

Illustrations and Captions

Illustrations and accompanying captions provide additional information to expand the reader's understanding. Illustrations provide a visual look at the information, and the captions explain what is being illustrated. In a section about tessellations, pictures of tiled floor designs might be used to illustrate the math concept. Illustrations provide additional information to enhance the reader's understanding and are a tremendous support to struggling readers who may experience difficulty reading the text but can still gather content information from the illustrations.

Index

The index, also in the back of the book, allows students to locate content within the text. Key items are listed in alphabetical order, with page numbers on which those topics are discussed. Students (or teachers) who want to find information about circumference, double-line graphs, or prime factorization can simply look up those words and find the page numbers on which those topics appear within the text.

Information in Margins

Textbooks often include additional information in the margins of each page. This information might include the lesson objective, key vocabulary, a related fact, or a materials list. Reading the information in the margins provides additional information or direction.

Lists or Bullets

While narrative text is written in paragraph form, content text frequently includes lists or bulleted items. The lists allow certain content to stand out and be easily read. Students are able to scan the text to quickly locate the ideas. Problem-solving strategies or units of measurement might be presented in a bulleted format.

Numeric Representations

Math textbooks often present numeric representations (e.g., algorithms) inset in the text or in a box near the text in which the algorithm is explained. These representations show the math idea in an abstract form using numbers and symbols to supplement the ideas in the text.

Table of Contents

The table of contents is in the front of the book and shows how the book is organized. Chapter titles provide a basic idea of topics, and page numbers are included for each chapter. If students are looking for information on a broad topic (e.g., ratios, rates, and proportions) checking the table of contents will allow them to locate the sections of their book that deal with that content. The table of contents also provides page numbers for the glossary, index, and other resource sections.

Text Clues

In content text, there may be clues within the words of the text to help students comprehend the meaning. Words like *first*, *next*, and *finally* help identify sequence. Words like *most important* might identify key ideas. Words like *same as*, *similar to*, *in contrast*, *different from*, and *rather than* might help students better understand compare-and-contrast statements. And *for instance* alerts students that an example will be used. Understanding these word clues helps students better understand the text.

CLASSROOM-TESTED TIP

Textbook Scavenger Hunt

Understanding the features of expository text can help students figure out ways to more clearly communicate about content. To help familiarize students with the features of expository text, send students on a scavenger hunt through their math textbooks. Design a series of questions, like the ones that follow, that require students to use the organization of the text (e.g., table of contents, index, glossary) and assist them in building math vocabulary and strengthening math concepts. Scavenger hunts are a great way to begin the year, as they help students get acquainted with their math books, or might be a nice activity to start a new standard, chapter, or math topic. These hunts can be done individually, but having students work in teams gets them talking about the math ideas.

Sample Questions

1. What is a histogram?

2. In which chapter can you learn about the Pythagorean Theorem?

3. What is the symbol for the absolute value of *x*?

4. Describe the diagram on page 213.

5. Define *corresponding angles*.

6. List the names of all the polygons on page 363.

7. On what pages might you learn about circle graphs?

8. In which chapter will you learn about ratios?

9. What is a *common factor* of a set of numbers?

10. What is a *dependent event*?

Supporting Struggling Readers

We know that many of the students in our classrooms are not reading on grade level, and while our long-range goal is to improve their reading skills, we realize that we also need to support them in decoding and understanding the math text and the written problems we assign in our daily lessons. So what can we do to support our students who struggle with reading even problem assignments?

The before-, during-, and after-reading strategies mentioned earlier in this chapter are critical for your struggling readers. Model the way in which you read the math book. Read the text, look at the pictures, and review the examples with students. Reinforce how, together, these features help you see the big ideas. Help your below-grade-level readers develop coping skills by reminding them to use picture clues whenever they are available. Perhaps there are sample problems that illustrate a procedure with numbers, so students can figure out how to proceed, or a graphic that helps clarify the words on the page.

Identify and review key vocabulary so your students are familiar with frequently used math words. The use of word walls and math vocabulary logs will give students continued exposure to important math words. Include frequent reviews of directional vocabulary. Do your students understand what it means to explain, justify, describe, illustrate, compare, reflect, categorize, list, organize, observe, analyze, evaluate, and draw conclusions? Review these terms and provide examples so your students will understand them when they see them in task directions.

When you are assessing students' understanding of math skills and concepts, try to separate the task of reading from the math task by reading directions to students or allowing students to read with a partner. Remember that reading aloud to students as they follow along or allowing students to read with a partner are ways we model and support students in developing their reading skills. When students become blocked by a word, encourage them to read through the word that they do not know. It may be that they can figure out the meaning of the sentence without knowing that word.

While many accountability assessments do not allow students to partner-read or do not allow you to read to your students, keep in mind that there is a critical difference between those assessments and your daily instruction. The decision was made, for accountability purposes, to test students without support, but daily instruction is about support. We scaffold learning by reading to students, allowing them to read along with others, guiding their reading, and then stepping back and giving them opportunities to try it on their own. For some assessments, they are on their own, but in our daily instruction, we are there to guide and support them as they develop their skills.

Differentiating the math task by using fewer words or simpler vocabulary may be appropriate for some students. Remember that the accompanying CD contains many writing tasks correlated to your content standards, and the editable format of the CD allows you to easily modify those tasks so they are at an appropriate reading level for your below-grade-level readers.

Regardless of the content area, the ability to read is fundamental in gathering information and accessing ideas. Despite our content teaching assignment, we are all teachers of reading. But being a teacher of reading does not mean that we spend our day teaching isolated reading skills. In our math classrooms, we teach reading skills on a daily basis through modeling our own reading strategies, supporting students with before-, during-, and after-reading strategies as they explore their math text, and helping them become more comfortable with the special features of expository text. Supporting our students as they read about mathematics helps minimize their anxiety and gives them tools to cope with the challenges of reading about math.

Questions for Discussion

1. How can math teachers prepare students to read math text? What before-reading strategies might be used?

2. How might math teachers support students in understanding and using the features of content text?

3. How can teachers support below-grade-level readers during math instruction?

4. In what ways might you collaborate with English/Language Arts teachers or school specialists to strengthen your students' skills in reading content text?

CHAPTER 8

Assessing Math Communication

Assessment of students and analysis of instruction are fundamentally interconnected.

—National Council of Teachers of Mathematics,
Professional Standards for Teaching Mathematics

What did assessment look like when you were a student in the math classroom? A chapter test? A unit test? A graded homework paper? What was the purpose of that assessment? To assign a grade? To determine if you passed or failed? When did it occur? When a unit of instruction was complete? In today's classrooms we have adjusted our vision of assessment and the role it can play to support learning. Rather than viewing it as a culminating activity to assess what has been learned, we view it as an ongoing activity, to gather information that helps us modify our teaching and enhance our students' learning. While we recognize that accountability testing (testing programs that result in scores to rank students, schools, or districts) is a part of our lives, this chapter focuses predominantly on classroom assessment—the assessment that we use each day to check our students' progress and modify our teaching to meet their needs.

Assessment and Communication

Ongoing assessment is integral to the teaching and learning process. It is through ongoing assessment that we are able to analyze our teaching practices, to recognize what is working and what needs to be modified in order to meet our students' needs. It is through ongoing assessment that we are able to identify what students have learned and find ways to help them extend their learning. Unlike the antiquated view of assessment as an end product, (e.g., chapter test that indicated whether we passed or failed) our current view of assessment is of ongoing and varied ways to gather information in order to teach in the most effective way possible and to help our students learn.

Certainly assessment helps to pinpoint where students are in their current understanding, but our hope is that it also leads to reflection about ways to enhance that understanding. In mathematics, understanding is measured by more than right or wrong answers. In order to assess our students' understanding we must know our students' thinking. Communication makes our students' thinking visible. By listening to students talk and reading what they have written, we are able to see the level to which they understand math ideas. We are able to identify misunderstandings and discover information that helps us design effective interventions.

In this chapter we explore ways to assess our students' math knowledge and skills through verbal and written communication, as well as ways to assess students' math communication skills. Through communication, we are able to see what our students know about mathematics. In addition, we recognize the important role that communication plays in helping students explore and express math ideas, so we strive to continually assess and strengthen their abilities to communicate mathematically.

A Look at Varied Assessments

Assessment is an ongoing process. We assess before we teach, to get an idea of where to begin. Then we teach, we assess, and we reteach, until our students have achieved their goals. Assessment can be formal (e.g., standardized tests, unit tests, accountability assessments) or it might be informal (e.g., observations, discussions, informal writing tasks). To be an integral component of our teaching, assessment must be frequent, appropriate to the skills we are teaching, and able to result in specific feedback to help our students improve their thinking.

Our goal is to determine what students know so that we can help them extend their understandings, so it is important that we are constantly assessing students in a variety of ways. We recognize that traditional math tests provide us with important information regarding whether students can find a correct solution, but we also recognize the value of alternate forms of assessment that provide us with more than just an answer. We can gather a great deal of information from listening to our students. By conducting whole-class discussions, we are able to hear our students' responses and gain greater insight into their thinking. When we stop and listen to our students' ideas, whether they are right or wrong, we gather data to guide our teaching.

A major value of group and partner work is that students must verbalize their ideas and when they are talking, we can listen. As we circulate through the classroom listening to small groups discuss their math ideas, we are able to identify strengths and misunderstandings. Many teachers like to carry a clipboard as they move through the room to jot down ideas or specific student comments that are overheard. Following the group activity, their notes help them clarify ideas or share one student's insights with the class.

Open-ended, or constructed-response, writing tasks provide us with valuable assessment data about students' understanding of a concept or skill. These tasks ask students for more than a number answer. Students are asked to explain, describe, summarize, or defend their math ideas (see Figure 8–1). When we ask students to write about math ideas, we are able to see the degree to which they understand those ideas. Are they beginning to get it? What is confusing them? We are able to see their misunderstandings, confusions, and insights.

Reviewing collections of student work provides opportunities to view our students' progress over time. Journals and portfolios are effective ways to store previous assignments in order to periodically review students' work to assess the gradual development of their skills. These tools allow us to notice progress that may not seem obvious to us on a day-to-day basis. For more on portfolios, see the Classroom-Tested Tip on this subject.

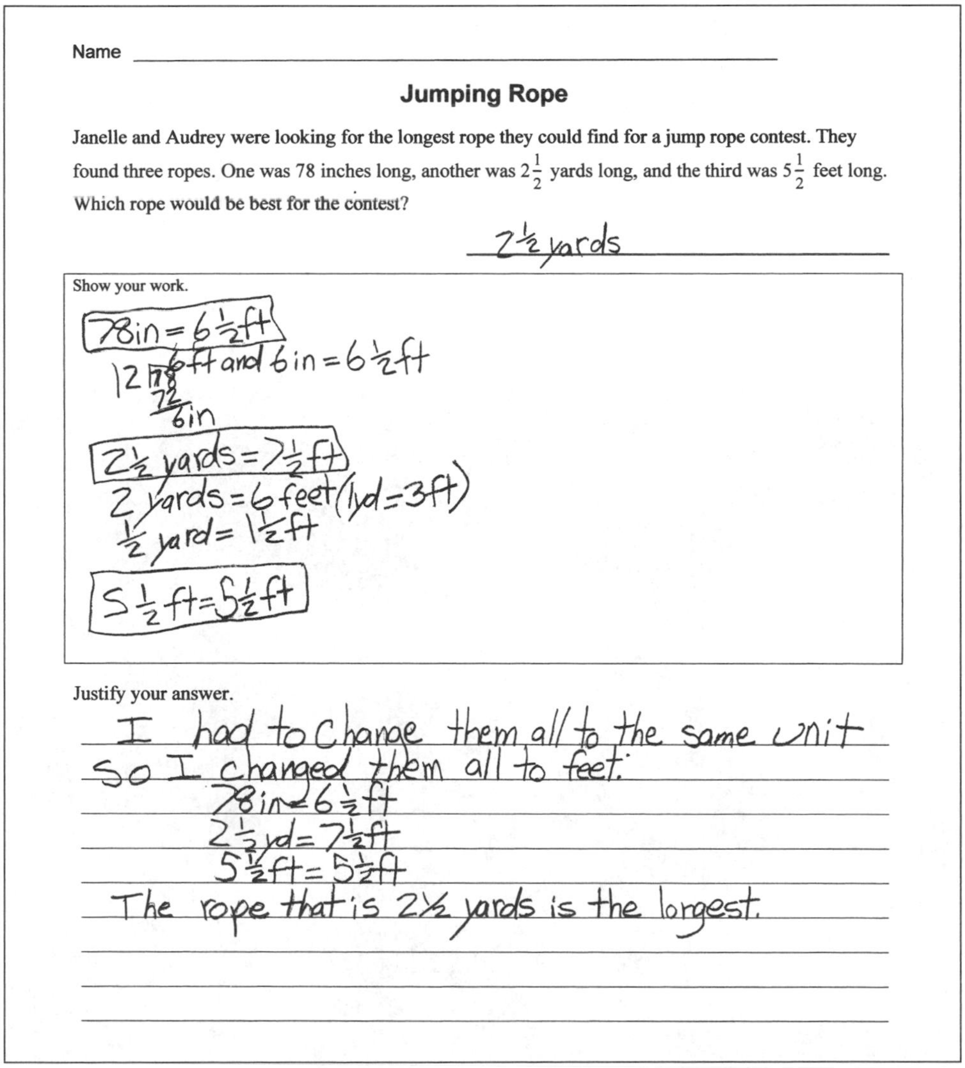
Name ______________________

Jumping Rope

Janelle and Audrey were looking for the longest rope they could find for a jump rope contest. They found three ropes. One was 78 inches long, another was $2\frac{1}{2}$ yards long, and the third was $5\frac{1}{2}$ feet long. Which rope would be best for the contest?

$2\frac{1}{2}$ yards

Show your work.

78in = $6\frac{1}{2}$ft
12)78 → 6 ft and 6 in = $6\frac{1}{2}$ft
72
6in
$2\frac{1}{2}$ yards = $7\frac{1}{2}$ft
2 yards = 6 feet (1yd = 3ft)
$\frac{1}{2}$ yard = $1\frac{1}{2}$ft
$5\frac{1}{2}$ft = $5\frac{1}{2}$ft

Justify your answer.

I had to Change them all to the same unit so I changed them all to feet.
78in = $6\frac{1}{2}$ft
$2\frac{1}{2}$yd = $7\frac{1}{2}$ft
$5\frac{1}{2}$ft = $5\frac{1}{2}$ft
The rope that is $2\frac{1}{2}$ yards is the longest.

Figure 8–1 *This student's writing and representations demonstrate his understanding of measurement concepts.*

Student interviews also provide data about student understanding. As we stop to ask individual students questions about their work, we are conducting informal interviews. We might ask them to explain how they solved a problem or to justify an answer or to clarify a part of their work. Their comments allow us to better assess their understanding of the skill.

Formal interviews, similar to writing conferences, can also provide valuable information (see Figure 8–2). Many teachers schedule brief conferences with students to hear more about their thinking. As the class is busy completing an assignment, the teacher chats with individual students to probe into their mathematical thinking. Using writing as a catalyst for these brief discussions works well. Ask your students to bring their writing to the conference. Have students read their writing to you and then discuss the ideas. Focus on assessing their understanding of the math ideas and providing tips for improving communication about those ideas. You might probe their math ideas with prompts like these:

Can you give me an example of what you mean?
How did you figure that out?
Why did you use those numbers?
Why did you use that operation?

Figure 8–2 *Brief writing conferences can provide a great deal of information on students' math understanding and communication skills.*

Or you might help them with communication skills through prompts directed at their writing:

What else might you say to help me understand that? (thoroughness, detail)
Is there a way you could make that clearer? (diagram, representations, organization of ideas)
Was there another way you could have said that? (vocabulary, word choice)

The use of a variety of assessment tools provides us with a more informed picture of our students' strengths and needs. Our goal is to gather a variety of data to assess our students' math understanding and communication skills, and then to use that data to improve both.

The Pros and Cons of Constructed-Response Assessments

In designing written assessments, we have format choices. After a lesson on subtracting decimals we might check our students' understanding in one of the following ways:

1. $1.5 - .03 =$

    a. 1.2

    b. .12

    c. 1.47

2. $1.5 - .03 = x$ Solve for x.

3. Marty says that $1.5 - .03 = 1.2$. Is he correct? Justify your answer.

Question 1 is in a multiple-choice format. Even when a correct answer is selected, there is no certainty that the student actually knows the answer. Question 2 is a computation. By asking students to solve for x, we can determine if their answer is right or wrong, but we cannot be sure of our students' understanding of what they have done. And then we have question 3, in which students are asked to justify their answer. In order to justify their decision about whether Marty's answer is correct, students must do the computation and compare their answer with Marty's. They must then verbalize their thinking. Michael said, "His answer isn't correct because he didn't line up the decimal points right. He needed to add a zero after the 1.5 so it was 1.50 and then subtract. He should have gotten 1.47. And it doesn't even make sense because .03 is a really small amount and subtracting it wouldn't change the number that much."

When students answer constructed-response questions, there are no choices to circle. The student must have an understanding of the concept and be able to express that understanding which is a more difficult task than a multiple-choice question or computation. Appropriate responses to our question will make us feel confident about our students' understanding. But what if our students respond in inaccurate ways?

> "It is correct because .5 − .03 = .2 so 1.5 − .03 = 1.2."

A frustrating part of assigning open-ended writing tasks is reviewing those tasks and seeing our students' misunderstandings. It is glaringly obvious when our students don't get it! But that is perhaps the greatest benefit of constructed-response tasks. Our goal is to figure out what they are thinking, even if it is not correct.

And back to our question about Marty's decimal subtraction. Sometimes we get responses that are so brief or so general that they don't shed much light on a student's thinking:

> "Marty didn't subtract right."

It may be that students don't understand the math and are saying as little as possible to mask their lack of knowledge. Or it may be that they can do the math, but their poor communication skills prohibit them from responding effectively. If they have difficulty expressing their ideas in writing, we often get short, general, or incomplete responses. Critical to our success with open-ended tasks as an assessment tool is our ability to help our students learn to communicate effectively about math. Do they know how to defend their ideas? When they can't find the words, do they know how to use pictures or examples to get their ideas on paper? Could they include labeled representations to help us understand their writing? Our assessment efforts must focus on both assessing the math ideas and improving the communication of those ideas.

The student work in Figures 8–3 and 8–4 shows different strengths and weaknesses and help us determine ways to support these students. The writing in Figure 8–3 indicates that this student does not understand which formula is appropriate for determining the surface area of a triangular prism. It is his math understanding that needs to be addressed, not his communication skills. In Figure 8–4, the student understands the mathematics, but her writing does not make that understanding clear. Instead of determining the area of the two triangle bases using the formula $A = 1/2bh$ for each one, she simply uses the formula $A = bh$ one time, after mentally combining the triangles. While this method is a very reasonable way to approach the task, her writing does not help us understand what she did. For this student, our focus will be on helping her communicate about what she has done, along with clarifying her error in labeling her answer.

When teaching for understanding, it is important to assess for understanding, which means going beyond number answers to probe the thinking behind those answers. Asking students to write is a way of getting at that thinking. Open-ended questioning helps us put the pieces together to figure out what might be going on within our students' heads. Not all math assessment needs to be open-ended, but recognizing the value of open-ended questioning to stimulate student thinking and to

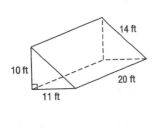

Using words, numbers, and or pictures, explain to your partner how you
would find the surface area of this triangular prism.

You would find the surface area of the triangular
prism by using the surface area formula, 2(lw)+
2(lh)+2(wh). To use this formula you have to know
what the length, width and height are. In the
end the formula will look like 2(20x11)+2(20x10)+
2(20x10) =

Figure 8–3 *This student inaccurately applies the formula for finding the surface area of a rectangular prism.*

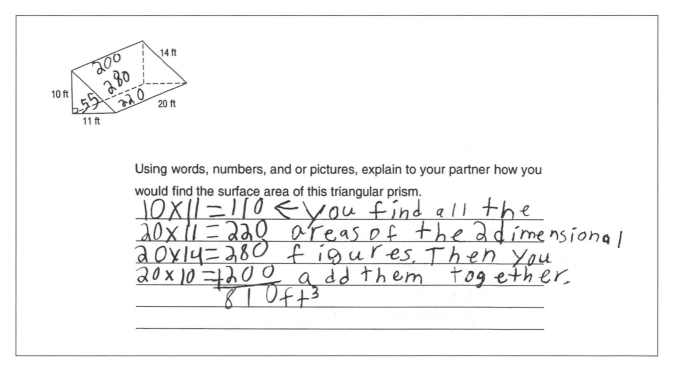

Using words, numbers, and or pictures, explain to your partner how you
would find the surface area of this triangular prism.

$10 \times 11 = 110$ ← You find all the
$20 \times 11 = 220$ areas of the 2 dimensional
$20 \times 14 = 280$ figures. Then you
$20 \times 10 = 200$ add them together.
$810 ft^3$

Figure 8–4 *This student does not clearly explain or label her computations, which could lead us to misunderstand her thinking.*

provide assessment data about that thinking, prompts us to incorporate these types of questions as a routine part of our assessment program.

The Unique Features of Writing About Math

Content writing, specifically writing about math, looks different from much of the writing we teach in language arts class. Look at your math textbook to see examples of writing about math.

- Numbers are okay, right in the middle of sentences!

    "There were 135 students at the basketball game."

- Symbols are okay; in fact, symbols are an important part of the language of math.

    "To find out how many CDs Ellen bought I did 4 × 5 because she bought 4 packs and each pack had 5 CDs in it."

- Incomplete sentences and labeled equations effectively convey math ideas.

    "3 (people) × $4.25 (cost of a ticket) = $12.75 (cost for everyone's tickets)"

- Representations (e.g., diagrams, tables, equations) often appear beside words to clarify and illustrate ideas.

    "Right triangles have one right angle like this."

- Lists can be as effective as paragraphs to communicate ideas.

    1. I multiplied 2 × $1.75 = $3.50 because I bought 2 bags of potato chips ($1.75 each).

    2. I added $3.50 + $2.45 because I also bought hot dogs ($2.45), so the total was $5.95.

    3. I rounded $5.95 to $6.00 and then divided it by 5 to figure out that we each owed about $1.20

- Important data might appear outside the sentences (e.g., computations in the *show your work* area), and combine with the words to clearly express the ideas.

To communicate math ideas effectively, writing about math may look a bit different from some other types of writing. The goal is to be able to express math ideas in an understandable way.

Writing as a Component to a Math Portfolio

Student portfolios have become a widely used tool for assessment and evaluation. Portfolios, unlike standardized tests, show the development of students' skills throughout the course of the year. Samples of student work are collected throughout the school year, students are given some input into the selection of work to be included in the portfolio, and self-reflection and goal-setting are essential components of the process.

While portfolios should contain a variety of ways in which students show their math understanding (e.g., projects, tests), writing tasks make a wonderful addition to a math portfolio. At intervals throughout the year (possibly quarterly), have students select a math writing task to be included in the portfolio and complete a self-reflection about the writing. Some possible reflective prompts might include the following:

- I could improve this piece of writing by . . .

- I received a score of ___ on this writing because . . .

- This writing assignment was difficult because. . . , but I learned . . .

- I am proud of this writing because . . .

- This writing shows that I can . . .

Have your students set goals for the next quarter. Students might be asked to list a goal related to math content and a goal related to math communication. Student goals might include adding more detail to written responses, explaining answers more fully, or using specific math vocabulary in their writing. Portfolio conferences are a wonderful time to talk with students about their goals and their reflections on their own work. Conferences can be informal (during class time) or formal (including parents at conference times).

The Role of Rubrics

We have seen the value of analyzing students' writing both to assess what they know and to clearly see what they don't know. But how do we score it? When an answer is either right or wrong it is quite easy to score the paper and quite easy to assign a specific score of 92 or 75 percent. But when we talk about scoring our students' writing about math, we recognize that the writing is not right or wrong. In fact, it probably has some right ideas mixed with some wrong ideas. And that makes sense, because we are now scoring students' thinking and that also has a mix of right and wrong as students move through the stages of developing math ideas.

Rubrics are a way to capture where a student's understanding falls on a continuum. If a score of 0 indicates no understanding and 4 indicates a full and complete understanding, then the range between them indicates students' progress toward understanding. Rubric scoring allows us to sort students' writing into categories based on the development of their thinking. We will never be able to assign a pinpoint score (82%) to students' thinking, but we can give it a ballpark score (0–4) to indicate a general stage of development. A look at some key adjectives used in rubrics reinforces the general nature of the scoring and illustrates the continuum of understanding:

in-depth	sufficient
thorough	fragmented
extensive	limited
clear	insufficient
appropriate	minimal
satisfactory	

It can be frustrating for us to use rubric scoring, particularly in math where we love pinpoint accuracy. It is important that we develop an understanding of the role of rubrics (to help us sort work across a continuum) and identify ways to better use rubrics (for our own assessment purposes and to help students improve their math and communication skills).

A multitude of rubrics are available to score students' writing about math. Some may be specific to a task (a scoring key), while others may be generic and applicable to almost any writing task. Select a rubric that makes sense to you, works with your task, and addresses the needs of your students.

Many rubrics assess both math ideas and communication skills. In order to score at the highest level, students must be able to accurately perform the math task and effectively explain their thinking. Figure 8–5 provides an example of a rubric for both content and communication.

Rubrics can be written with student-friendly language. The rubric in Figure 8–6 speaks directly to students.

Some rubrics are very brief and score for a complete understanding, a minimal understanding, or a lack of understanding, as in Figure 8–7.

Content and Communication Rubric

    4 – Answer is correct and complete; clear and thorough explanation.
    3 – Answer may contain minor errors; explanation is sufficient.
    2 – Answer is partially correct; explanation may be insufficient.
    1 – Answer is incorrect; explanation is unclear.
    0 – No attempt made.

Figure 8–5 *This generic rubric assesses students' knowledge of content and their ability to communicate that knowledge.*

Scoring Rubric with Student-Friendly Language

4 – Your answer is completely correct, and your explanation is clear.

3 – Your answer contains a minor mistake that you can fix on your own.

– or –

Your answer is correct, but your explanation is unclear.

2 – You made progress toward a correct solution, but you made an error that shows you need to continue to develop your skills on this type of problem.

1 – There are major mistakes in your work, or your work shows that you do not understand the problem or how to solve it.

0 – You didn't try to solve the problem.

Figure 8–6 *Rubrics that are directed to your students, with language such as "your explanation" and "your answer," help students focus on their own progress.*

Brief Scoring Rubric

2 - Your response demonstrates a complete understanding and analysis of the problem.

■ Your answer is correct.

■ You applied a reasonable strategy.

■ Your explanation and/or justification is clear, developed, and logical.

■ Supporting numbers and information are provided as appropriate.

1 - Your response demonstrates a minimal understanding and analysis of the problem.

■ Your answer may contain some errors.

■ You partially applied a reasonable strategy.

■ Your explanation and/or justification is partially developed, logically flawed, or missing.

■ Supporting numbers and information may be missing.

0 – Your response is completely incorrect or missing.

Figure 8–7 *This rubric is on a 0–2 scale, but scores for content and math communication.*

While our hope is that all student work can be sorted into one of the rubric categories, we do sometimes find a work sample that may be difficult to fit into the categories. Do your best. Rubrics are meant to support you in identifying the level of your students' thinking, but students can sometimes surprise us with thinking that is unusual and hard to assess. Find the score that best fits the work, but consider gathering additional data to clarify your understanding of the students' skills through talking with students or closely observing their next assignment.

The Value of More Specific Rubrics

While generic rubrics are valuable in that they can be used with nearly all types of writing, there are times when students benefit from feedback that is more specific. If you are working on math communication skills and want to support students as they learn to explain how they got an answer, you might try a rubric like the one in Figure 8–8. A critical component of explaining the process includes outlining the steps taken to solve the problem. This rubric reminds students of important components of this writing and allows us to assess the development of specific communication skills. For additional rubrics, see the CD.

Rubrics can be effective tools for scoring student writing. The selection of an appropriate rubric allows us to guide students' writing by using it as a preview tool, to assess students' writing following the task, and to share specific feedback to help students improve their math and communication skills.

Rubric for Writing to Explain a Process

4 – Explanation is clear. A logical sequence is thoroughly presented and in a reasonable order. For problem solving, the writing shows a clear connection between the steps taken to solve the problem and the problem situation.

3 – Explanation is generally clear. There may be minor flaws in the sequencing or minor steps may be missing. For problem solving, it is generally apparent how the steps connect to the problem situation.

2 – Explanation is somewhat clear. There may be significant flaws in the sequencing or important steps may be missing. It may be unclear how the steps connect to the problem situation.

1 – Explanation lacks clarity. Sequence is nonexistent or difficult to follow and does not include important steps. It is unclear how the steps connect to the problem situation.

0 – Blank, no response.

Figure 8–8 *This rubric guides students as they write to explain how they solved a problem.*

CLASSROOM-TESTED TIP

Using Rubrics to Support Students

Along with providing accountability data (e.g., report card grades) and informing us of students' level of math understanding, rubric scoring is a way to help our students better understand our expectations. Provide frequent opportunities for your students to explore rubric scoring. Show rubrics to students prior to the task to focus their attention on what is expected. Following writing tasks, rubrics provide students with feedback about their writing. Help your students feel comfortable with your rubrics with activities like the following:

- Show students how you assess their writing. Put a sample student response on the overhead projector or video visualizer. Score it as you think aloud. "Do I understand the math ideas? Is the vocabulary appropriate? Is the order correct? Are there enough examples? Is it clearly written?" Talk it through as students watch and listen. Do another one with student input. Have them talk it through with you.

- Get students involved in scoring. Put some student writing samples on the overhead projector or video visualizer and read them to the class. Provide students with number cards (0, 1, 2, 3, or 4) and ask them to hold up the number to indicate the score they would give each response. Have students justify their scores to see if they clearly understand the rubric. Or provide a sample student response and ask students to score it in pairs or groups. Students should discuss and agree on a score. Have pairs or groups justify their scores to the class.

Managing the Assessment of Math Writing

Writing serves a variety of purposes. At times we ask students to record their ideas simply to help them formalize their thinking, to get their ideas out of their heads and onto the paper so they can see and revise them. At other times, we want students to describe a concept so that we can assess their math understanding of that concept. We may be teaching a math process and ask students to record the process so they will internalize the ideas. Not all math writing must be formally scored. Consider your purpose in assigning the task to determine the type of feedback that is most appropriate.

You might read students' writing as you circulate through the room and offer impromptu verbal assistance. Some writing is developmental writing, helping students refine their skills. After a writing task, you might simply discuss the writing with the whole class, commenting on key math ideas that would have strengthened the response or sharing writing tips that might have made their writing clearer. When writing is meant to spark math ideas, you might have students read their work with a partner and compile a combined response to read aloud. Score student writing frequently enough to keep abreast of their individual progress and provide them with individual feedback, but remember that writing is a tool for developing math understanding and not all writing needs to be polished and scored to achieve that goal.

A Note About Language Mechanics

Language conventions (e.g., spelling, grammar, punctuation) help make our writing understandable. They are tools to help us, not restrictions to tie us down. Be careful they don't restrict your students when they are taking on the tough task of writing about math. Will marking misspelled words persuade them to use safer words that are less mathematically appropriate (e.g., *side* rather than *hypotenuse*)? Will worrying about indenting paragraphs distract them from the math ideas they are struggling to convey? Decide on what is important to assess. Most likely you will want to focus on assessing what your students know about math and how well they are able to express those ideas. Put away your red pen as they are developing their math writing skills. Allow them to write ideas in a relaxed and supportive atmosphere and help them learn to clarify those ideas (an important language arts skill). Remember that when students are writing about complex content, with a technical language including numbers and symbols, the expression of ideas can be a challenge. If you should decide to incorporate language mechanics in your scoring and expectations, be sure to allow time for proofreading. The writing process always begins with the brainstorming of ideas, continues on to the revision of those ideas in order to clarify content, and finally, finishes up with the proofreading to polish the work.

Writing About Math on Accountability Testing

We are all quite aware that today's high-stakes accountability testing programs frequently ask our students to write about their math thinking through brief constructed-response tasks and sometimes extended writing tasks. First and foremost, this is a recognition that math knowledge is about more than right answers and rote procedures. Our students are expected to be able to explain, defend, and describe their math ideas.

These tests are scored outside of our school buildings, by impartial reviewers, so the clarity of our students' writing becomes critical. These reviewers have no reference point to say, "Oh, but Jason understands measurement. I know what he meant to say." Instead they are forced to score Jason's work based on what he *did* say—the words that are on the paper in front of them. Our attention to developing our students' communication skills becomes critical for their success on these assessments.

The constructed-response items on these tests are scored primarily for math content rather than for writing elements. Students, however, must have the ability to clearly convey their math ideas in writing, and they benefit tremendously from the routine use of writing as an instructional tool in the math classroom. Although the test items are often shorter than many instructional tasks, the goal remains for students to be able to express their math ideas through clear, concise, and organized writing.

While the administration of the tests does not generally allow direct support, students benefit greatly from support during instruction. Many of the instructional techniques we have focused on throughout this book will benefit our students as they engage in these high-stakes assessments.

■ *Teacher questioning and think-alouds:* Students begin to internalize the questions they must ask themselves as they write independently.

■ *Vocabulary development:* Many brief constructed-response tests provide limited space for students to write, making word choice a critical way for them to clearly and concisely express their math ideas.

■ *Classroom discussions:* Classroom discussions allow students to hear others' responses (both the content and the way in which they express that content), and also give students a chance to orally practice formulating their own responses.

■ *Attention to the organization of writing (e.g., supporting details, order of ideas, transition words):* While most math assessments do not assess for specific writing elements, instruction in those writing conventions supports students' ability to organize their thoughts and express them in a way that the reader (scorer) understands. The ability to write ideas in a logical order allows the reader to follow along as he or she reads the response. The use of a topic sentence focuses the writer and the reader on the content that will follow. And while the inclusion of a topic sentence may not be necessary to receive a high score, it may be helpful in focusing students on the task ahead.

■ *Attention to various types of writing (e.g., writing to explain how or to justify why):* Whether we are writing extended tasks or short responses, we write for various purposes. If questions ask students to explain *how*, they must identify the steps they performed, but if asked to justify *why*, they should recognize the importance of including math data or reasoning to support their answer. Understanding the question is a key to correctly answering it.

■ *Improving writing through the sharing of student work samples:* Class discussions and the sharing of student samples allow students to see ways to improve their responses to ensure that they are correct and complete. Discussions might include the reasoning behind decisions about the use of words, pictures, numbers, or some combination of those to effectively express the math ideas.

There are no shortcuts to scoring high on constructed-response math items. Your students' response will depend on their understanding of the math skill or concept *and* their ability to communicate their ideas. Students who learn math in a classroom filled with communication have the advantage of exploring math ideas and developing deep understandings through their discussions and writing. In addition, students who regularly write about their math ideas and are consistently supported to improve their communication skills will be better prepared to show what they know through writing.

Communication, both oral and written, provides us with invaluable information to assess our students' understanding, guide their progress, and adjust and monitor our teaching. By listening to our students' comments and analyzing their written work, we are better able to support and guide them in understanding math ideas.

Questions for Discussion

1. What role does communication play in assessing students' math understanding?

2. Why is it important to use varied approaches to assessment?

3. What are the advantages and challenges of rubric scoring?

4. How might an understanding of rubrics help prepare students for a writing task (preview tool) and provide feedback about a writing task (review tool)?

CHAPTER 9

Communication Across the Content Standards

Teachers are responsible for the quality of the mathematical tasks in which students engage. Teachers should choose and develop tasks that are likely to promote the development of students' understandings of concepts and procedures in a way that fosters their ability to solve problems and to reason and communicate mathematically.

—National Council of Teachers of Mathematics,
Professional Standards for Teaching Mathematics

Thus far, we have seen that communication, although it is a critical process skill, does not stand alone. It is connected to other processes through which students learn and explore math ideas. The NCTM Process Standards (2000) of problem solving, communication, representation, reasoning and proof, and connections describe critical processes that are intertwined in our math lessons. As students communicate, they are able to analyze and explore problem situations. They combine their written and verbal skills with representation skills to better express and represent their ideas. They process their reasoning and express convincing arguments both orally and in writing, and they explore the many connections between and among math ideas. These five process standards interconnect in daily lessons as we develop and refine math content with our students.

While there is much overlap between the process standards, there must also be a strong connection between the process and content standards. Communication is a process through which students learn math content and through which they are able to express their ideas. Providing students with experiences that allow them to talk and write about mathematics in various content areas is a critical way to help students practice application of these skills as well as to promote active engagement with math content. The National Council of Teachers of Mathematics (2000) has outlined the content standards for middle grades students and has organized those standards in five content areas: number and operations, algebra, measurement, geometry, and data analysis and probability. While we help students develop their skills in the processes of problem solving, reasoning and proof, communication, representation, and connections, we are also focused on building their understanding of this content. This chapter explores the interconnectedness of the content and process standards through sample lessons that illustrate a blending of content and process. Resources to support you in implementing these activities are available on the CD.

Communicating About Number and Operations

Students in grades 6 through 8 are exploring relationships between numbers and the ways in which numbers are represented. They are expected to understand the concepts of fractions and percents, including ways to represent each one and the ability to convert from one to the other. In addition, they are expected to understand how to connect these concepts to other mathematical ideas (e.g., area). In the following lesson, sixth-grade students were challenged to create a color tile design and then determine the fractional parts and percentages of each color in their design.

The Activity

Mr. Downey began the lesson by posing a problem to his sixth-grade class.

> **The floor in Vinny's Video Arcade is black, and Vinny would like to brighten it with a colorful rug. Use color tiles to design a rug for the arcade floor. Your rug must have 4 colors and can have an area of no more than 30 square tiles.**

Students were given square tiles in four colors and asked to work with partners to design a rug based on the problem scenario. Partners were asked to then color their rug design on grid paper and determine the fractional parts of their rug that were red, blue, yellow, and green. Mr. Downey asked each pair to raise their hands when they had completed the task. As pairs raised their hands, he met with each pair and asked them to explain how they arrived at their answers. One student shared, "We just counted the number of tiles and it was our denominator and then however many tiles were that color was our numerator." Mr. Downey asked questions of the students, having one pair explain why their fractions did not have the same denominators (they had simplified some of the fractions). As pairs explained their process and justified their answers to Mr. Downey's satisfaction, he challenged them with the second part of the task: determining the percentage of each color on their rug.

Again, Mr. Downey asked the pairs to raise their hands when they had found their answers. Students worked at various speeds, so some pairs were determining percentages while others were still working on the fractional parts. He again questioned the students to be sure they understood the process of determining the percentages.

MR. DOWNEY: How did you figure out the percents?

STUDENT: We just made the denominator 100.

MR. DOWNEY: Why did you do that?

STUDENT: Because a percent is how many out of 100 and there weren't 100 of any of the colors, so we did equivalent fractions to make them out of 100.

MR. DOWNEY: How can you be sure that your answers are correct? How might you check your answers?

STUDENT: We could add them and see if they equal 100%.

MR. DOWNEY: Why would they equal 100%?

STUDENT: Because 100% would be all of the colors together because 100% is the whole amount when you have percents.

After informally interviewing students to verify their understanding, Mr. Downey asked them to work together to write an explanation of how they determined the percentages for each color. Most pairs collaborated before beginning to write their joint explanation, but Kara and Steve began writing silently on their own papers. Mr. Downey reminded them to talk about their method, prompting them to read aloud what they had written so far, and he asked them to work together to create one "outstanding explanation".

Finally, several pairs were asked to present their rug designs to the class and describe their methods for determining the percentage of each color. Mr. Downey gave each student an index card and asked the class to listen carefully because they would be writing one thing they learned after listening to the presentations. He selected several pairs to share their methods, being sure to select pairs who did the task in different ways (i.e., finding equivalent fractions with a denominator of 100 or dividing the numerator by the denominator). Kelly and Lee used both methods, as they explained in their writing (see Figure 9–1). Mr. Downey collected the index cards and shared some of the students' insights with the class.

About the Math

In this lesson, as students created rug designs they reviewed and refined their understanding of area, their ability to identify fractional parts, their ability to create equivalent fractions, and their understanding of procedures for converting fractions to percents. They sharpened their reasoning skills as they determined a method for checking the reasonableness of their answers. By posing a task that required students to apply many math skills, the teacher was able to review skills for those who needed additional exposure to the ideas, as well as assess his students' understanding of the math skills and concepts.

Students explored and expressed their understandings about numbers in both verbal and written ways. Students were frequently asked to explain their thinking, whether it involved describing how they determined the fractions and percents of the colors in their rug designs or justifying how they knew those answers were correct. They were asked to produce collaborative writing about their approaches, and some students presented their methods to the class in order to share different procedures.

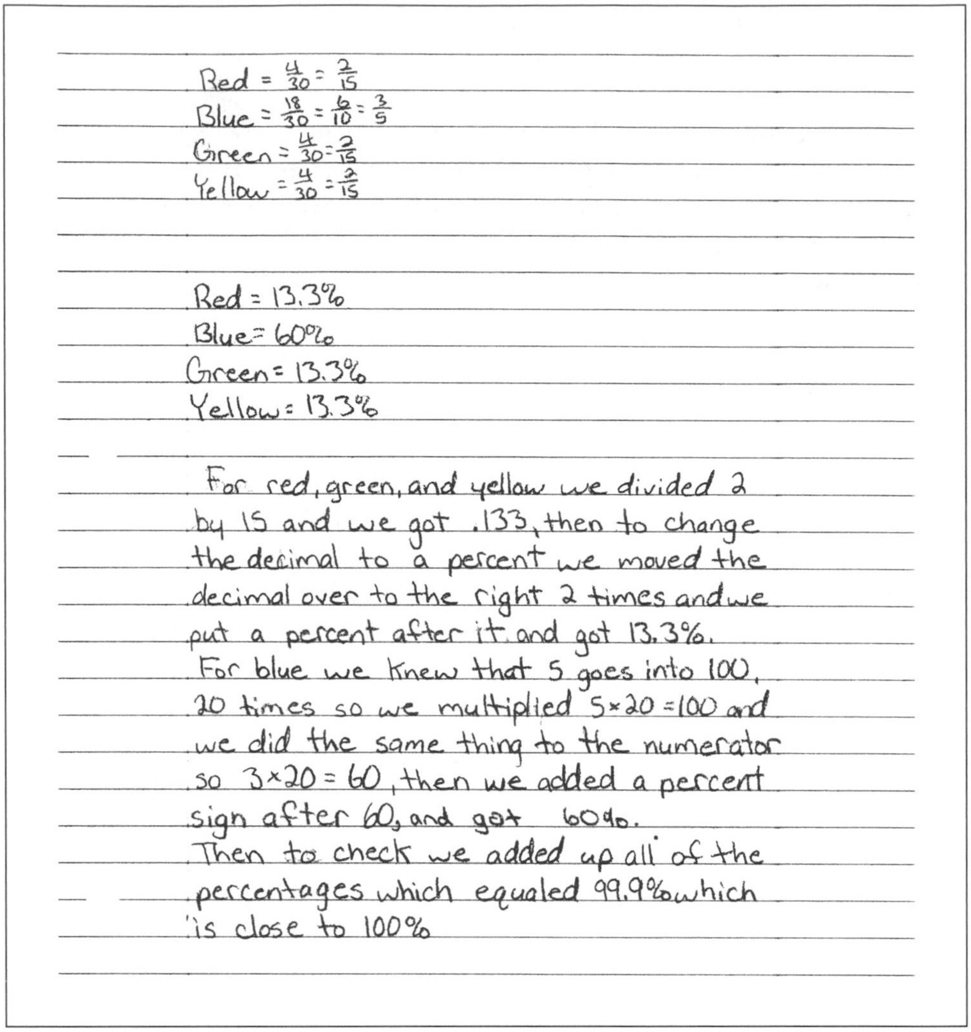

$$Red = \frac{4}{30} = \frac{2}{15}$$
$$Blue = \frac{18}{30} = \frac{6}{10} = \frac{3}{5}$$
$$Green = \frac{4}{30} = \frac{2}{15}$$
$$Yellow = \frac{4}{30} = \frac{2}{15}$$

Red = 13.3%
Blue = 60%
Green = 13.3%
Yellow = 13.3%

For red, green, and yellow we divided 2
by 15 and we got .133, then to change
the decimal to a percent we moved the
decimal over to the right 2 times and we
put a percent after it and got 13.3%.
For blue we knew that 5 goes into 100,
20 times so we multiplied 5×20 = 100 and
we did the same thing to the numerator
so 3×20 = 60, then we added a percent
sign after 60, and got 60%.
Then to check we added up all of the
percentages which equaled 99.9% which
is close to 100%

Figure 9–1 *This student explains how she and her partner determined their percentages and why they are sure that their answers are correct.*

To keep everyone engaged in the presentations, students were asked to record an idea they learned, and those ideas were shared with the class to bring closure to the lesson.

The teacher was able to differentiate instruction by having students work in pairs, and then moving through the classroom to pose specific questions to pairs of students. Pairs were asked to raise their hands as they finished a task, allowing each pair to work at their own pace and allowing the teacher to support them with questions appropriate to their level of understanding. While fast-moving students proceeded to the second part of the task, other pairs were receiving guidance and support with the initial part of the problem. Through the process of communication, students had repeated opportunities to refine their math thinking, get support as they continued to develop their understanding, and express their ideas to the teacher and their classmates.

Communicating About Algebra

Students in grades 6 through 8 are expected to be able to use tables and graphs to represent and analyze change. Students are refining their skills at observing change and determining how change in one variable is related to change in another. In the following lesson, eighth-grade students were challenged to collect data, create a scatterplot, and determine the line of best fit.

The Activity

Mrs. Smith began the lesson by giving each student a piece of licorice, a ruler, and a piece of graph paper. She asked the students to measure their piece of licorice in centimeters, and then to record their results on a table like the following:

Bites	0										
Length (cm)	20										

Most students found that the licorice was about 20 cm at the start of the task. Students were then asked to take a bite and again measure and record their data. The students were asked to continue that process until their licorice was gone. Mrs. Smith circulated through the room to observe as students began biting, measuring, and recording.

After the students completed the task, Mrs. Smith asked them to compare their data with a partner. Most students had recorded similar data. Mrs. Smith began asking questions about the data.

MRS. SMITH: Which part of your data is the independent variable?
STUDENT: The number of bites.
MRS. SMITH: Why?
STUDENT: Because that was what I controlled and nothing else could affect it.
MRS. SMITH: What is the dependent variable?
STUDENT: The length of the licorice.
MRS. SMITH: Why?
STUDENT: Because the length depended on how many bites I took.
MRS. SMITH: What kind of graph should we choose to display this data?
STUDENT: A line graph.
STUDENT: I don't think a line graph would be the best choice because not all bites were the same size, so the data is not constant.
MRS. SMITH: Any other ideas?
STUDENT: We could do a scatterplot so we could plot the points for the pairs of data.
MRS. SMITH: What do you mean when you say "pairs of data"?
STUDENT: The number of bites and the length of the licorice.

The class agreed to create a scatterplot, but before the students began plotting their data, Mrs. Smith asked them to predict whether the data would show a positive (rising) relationship, negative (falling) relationship, or no relationship. Darrell said it would be negative because "as the number of bites increases, the size of the licorice decreases." With thumbs-up approval, the class agreed with Darrell.

After the data points were plotted, Mrs. Smith asked the students to use their rulers to draw the line of best fit to see the correlation between the variables, and then to analyze the data from the line to identify the slope, y-intercept, and x-intercept, asking various students to clarify how they might determine each of those numbers. Molly explained that she would find the x-intercept by looking at "where the line crosses the x axis." "What would be the value of y?" Mrs. Smith asked. Molly said, "$y = 0$." Jenna shared the formula for finding the slope. After this quick review, students got to work determining their answers.

When students had finished, they recorded their data on the board in order to compare it. Suzanne asked if students were incorrect if they did not have the same answers, but most agreed that they would be correct. Michael explained that the reason was that "they take different-size bites, so that would change the slope and also the number of bites (x-intercept) they would have to take to finish." While there were slight variations, students noticed the negative correlation in all of their scatterplots.

Using the data from the line, students were asked to write the equation for the line of best fit. Students were asked to explain their work to a partner. Partners that did not agree were asked to raise their hands so Mrs. Smith could join their discussions. Finally, students entered the data from their table into a graphing calculator to find the line of best fit, and compared it to their answers. Mrs. Smith circulated through the room, checking the accuracy of students' work and asking questions to be sure they understood both the manual and calculator methods.

Finally, Mrs. Smith asked students to work in teams to prepare a "tips list" for students who might need to know how to construct a scatterplot, analyze the correlation, and find a line of best fit. Teams reported their "tips" as Mrs. Smith compiled a class list to summarize the lesson.

About the Math

In this lesson, students were challenged to gather data, record it on tables, graph it, and find the line of best fit. They were challenged to analyze their data by determining the slope, y-intercept, and x-intercept. Students contemplated the type of graph that might be best for their data, and were given opportunities to graph the data manually as well as with a graphing calculator.

While students gathered and graphed individual data, the teacher gave them many opportunities to compare and discuss their data with classmates. The teacher continually moved through the room listening to students' conversations to monitor their progress, and when partners could not agree on solutions, she joined their conversations to clarify important ideas. To summarize key ideas, she asked students to create "tips" lists and compiled their ideas to bring closure to the lesson.

Communicating About Geometry

An expectation for students in grades 6 through 8 is the ability to describe geometric shapes and recognize geometric relationships. They are refining observation skills as they look for formulas to make sense of geometric relationships (e.g., the relationship between the measures of sides of right triangles). In the following lesson, seventh-grade students engaged in an interactive lesson to develop their conceptual understanding of the Pythagorean Theorem.

The Activity

To begin the lesson, Mrs. Birch gave her students centimeter grid paper and asked them to draw a right angle on the paper. She told students they would be creating a triangle by finding and marking a point on each of the angle's rays (measuring 3 cm from the vertex on one ray and 4 cm from the vertex on the other) and then connecting those points to form a triangle. Mrs. Birch asked students to tell her what kind of triangle they had created, and Jessie responded that it was a right triangle. "How do you know?" Mrs. Birch asked. "Because we started with a right angle," Jessie explained. Mrs. Birch continued questioning the class.

MRS. BIRCH: How long are the first two sides you drew?
STUDENT: 3 centimeters and 4 centimeters
MRS. BIRCH: How do you know?
STUDENT: I counted them.
MRS. BIRCH: Do you remember what we call those sides on a right triangle?
No response.
MRS. BIRCH: Can you find it on our word wall? There is a special name for the two
    sides that connect to the right angle.
STUDENT: Legs
MRS. BIRCH: That's right, and what do we call the side opposite the right angle?
STUDENT: Hypotenuse
MRS. BIRCH: Can you show me the legs and hypotenuse on this right triangle? (*She
    draws a right triangle on the board.*)

A student approached the board and correctly identified the legs and hypotenuse. Mrs. Birch then asked the students to point to the hypotenuse of their right triangle and watched as they located the hypotenuse.

MRS. BIRCH: How long is the hypotenuse?
(No students answered.)
MRS. BIRCH: Can you tell by counting?
STUDENT: No.
MRS. BIRCH: Why not?

STUDENT: It's going diagonally.

MRS. BIRCH: Give me an estimate of what it might measure.

STUDENT: More than 3 cm because it's longer than the 3 cm side.

STUDENT: I think about 5 cm or 6 cm because it looks longer than either of the legs.

Mrs. Birch then asked her students to begin at the leg of the triangle that was 3 centimeters and to construct a square on their grid paper that was 3 centimeters on all sides. She also asked them to create a square that was 4 centimeters on each side using the 4 cm leg of the triangle as one side of their square.

MRS. BIRCH: How many squares on the grid are within the small square you created?

STUDENT: Nine.

MRS. BIRCH: How many squares on the grid are within the larger square you created?

STUDENT: Sixteen.

Mrs. Birch asked the students to turn to a partner and talk about what they noticed about those numbers and what they noticed when they found the sum of those numbers. Students talked in pairs and Mrs. Birch listened to their conversations as they began to recognize that the numbers (9, 16) were square numbers and that their sum was also a square number (25). Mrs. Birch then asked students to draw a square that had a total of 25 square centimeters (the sum of the units from the two triangles they had created) on a separate part of their grid paper and then to cut it out and place one side of it along the hypotenuse (the "unknown" side) of their triangle. As students set their 5 cm × 5 cm square next to the hypotenuse Mrs. Birch heard their excitement through comments like "Perfect match!" and "It fits!"

Mrs. Birch then asked her students to create a right triangle with legs that were 6 and 8 centimeters, to again create squares starting from each leg, and to create a square that was the sum of the units in the two squares they created. She asked them to turn to a partner and predict what might happen when they placed the new square along the hypotenuse. She moved through the room observing them and listening to their discussions. Then she asked one pair to describe what happened, placing their triangle and squares on a video visualizer, so the class could both see and hear their ideas.

"So what if I did not have a grid so that I could cut out squares? Can you find a way we can figure out the length of the hypotenuse without actually making the squares?" she asked. Students talked together and then shared their ideas. Emily volunteered, "You just square the legs and it equals the hypotenuse squared." Many students nodded in agreement.

Mrs. Birch shared that a famous mathematician, Pythagoras, discovered this long ago as he was working with right triangles, so the formula is named for him (the Pythagorean Theorem). She paraphrased Emily's ideas adding that we could call the legs a and b and the hypotenuse could be c, so

$$a^2 + b^2 = c^2$$

Mrs. Birch continued to ask questions:

MRS. BIRCH: What if we know the hypotenuse, but not the measure of one of the legs?
STUDENT: We could go backward and figure it out.
MRS. BIRCH: Can you give me an example?
STUDENT: If we knew that a leg was 3 units and the hypotenuse was 5 units, then we could substitute and say 3 squared + b squared = 5 squared and figure it out.

Mrs. Birch moved to the blackboard and began to write the equation. "Will that work?" she asked as she modeled solving the equation.

$$3^2 + b^2 = 5^2$$
$$9 + b^2 = 25$$
$$b^2 = 16$$
$$b = 4$$

Mrs. Birch said, "It works! Our formula is pretty handy!"

Mrs. Birch then gave each student a drawing of a right triangle with measurements for one leg and for the hypotenuse (see template on the CD), this time asking students to work independently to find the length of the missing leg. She reminded students that they should justify their answers on their paper. "What do I mean when I say *justify*?" she asked. "Prove it," said Taylor. "Don't just put the answer," said Bob. Mrs. Birch clarified her instructions: "Remember you can use numbers, words, or symbols to prove your answer. Convince me that your answer is correct." As students worked, she moved through the room observing and asking questions of some students to guide their thinking (see Figure 9–2). Mrs. Birch collected their work to assess their understanding, and then she asked students to summarize some of the important ideas from the lesson. Students mentioned the formula, the understanding of squaring sides, the theorem named for Pythagoras, and the ability to find the length of either the legs or the hypotenuse.

About the Math

In this lesson, students created right triangles, reviewed key vocabulary including vertex, leg, and hypotenuse, and explored square numbers. The teacher engaged students in a hands-on task to develop the concept of the Pythagorean Theorem and asked students to determine a generalization or formula based on their observations.

Throughout the task, students had opportunities to talk with partners, to hear other students' ideas as they presented their work, to see teacher modeling, and to work independently. The teacher frequently asked the students to explain their thinking and allowed students to show their work using a visualizer so that all students could see the work as they explained their ideas. At the end of the lesson, asking students to complete a task independently and justify their answer allowed the teacher

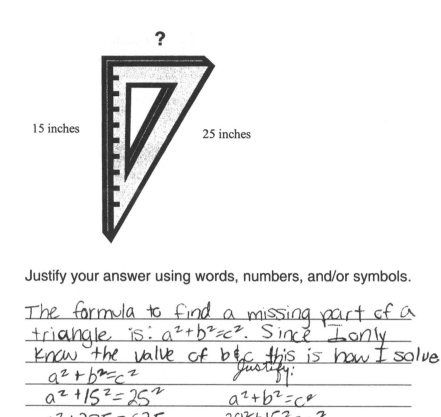

Given this triangle, find the length of the missing leg.

?

15 inches

25 inches

Justify your answer using words, numbers, and/or symbols.

The formula to find a missing part of a triangle is: $a^2 + b^2 = c^2$. Since I only know the value of b & c this is how I solve:

$a^2 + b^2 = c^2$

$a^2 + 15^2 = 25^2$

$a^2 + 225 = 625$

-225

$a^2 = \sqrt{400}$

$a = 20$ inches

Justify:

$a^2 + b^2 = c^2$

$20^2 + 15^2 = c^2$

$400 + 225 = c^2$

$\sqrt{625} = c^2$

$25 = c$

Figure 9–2 *This student first shows how she found the answer and then justifies her answer by substituting it into the equation.*

to assess their understanding of the geometry concept as well as their ability to adequately justify their answer. Asking students to summarize key ideas provided lesson closure.

Communicating About Measurement

Students in sixth through eighth grades are expected to identify and understand formulas for determining the surface area of a variety of three-dimensional figures. Students connect their understanding of finding the area of the two-dimensional faces of three-dimensional figures in order to calculate the surface area. In the following lesson, sixth graders engaged in hands-on explorations of surface area of a rectangular prism in order to expand their understanding of the formula.

The Activity

To begin the lesson, Mrs. Partin showed her sixth-grade students a box of cookies. "What shape is this?" she asked, and students confirmed that it was a rectangular prism. She then picked up a sheet of paper and asked students to compare and contrast the cookie box (rectangular prism) and the sheet of copy paper (rectangle), asking them to share ideas with a partner. Students commented that one was a rectangle and the other had a face that was a rectangle, that one was a quadrilateral and the other was made of quadrilaterals, and that they both had corners with 90-degree angles. They also commented that the rectangular prism was three-dimensional, while the rectangle was two-dimensional.

Mrs. Partin then asked students to visualize the cookie box if it were cut and flattened into a two-dimensional shape. She cut the box at several edges and flattened it to create a net, asking students to describe it to her. They mentioned that it was made of 6 rectangles, but the discussion was diverted for several minutes as they discussed whether squares were rectangles, finally agreeing that "all squares were rectangles because they all have 4 sides, 4 right angles, and their opposite sides are parallel, but not all rectangles are squares because to be a square you also need the four sides to be congruent." Mrs. Partin then gave each student a net that would form a rectangular prism, but this prism was configured differently from the net she had created by cutting the cookie box (see Figure 9–3).

She asked the students to turn to a partner and predict the three-dimensional shape that would be created by the net, and then asked them to cut out the net and create the figure. Students cut and taped the net to create rectangular prisms. Mrs. Partin prompted students to think about the prisms they had created.

"How many faces does a rectangular prism have?"
"If I change it to a two-dimensional net, how many rectangles should I have?"

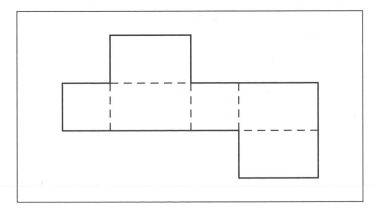

Figure 9–3 *Net for rectangular prism.*

"When you compared this net to the net of the cookie box, what do you notice
  about the number of rectangles?"
"What makes the two nets different? How are they the same?"

Mrs. Partin told the students they would be finding the surface area of the rectangular prism, asking a student to remind her what that meant. Shauna said, "It is the area of all of the faces." "So how will it help us to know that a rectangular prism is made of 6 rectangles?" Mrs. Partin asked. "Then we can just find the area of each rectangle," Darnell said. "How will you do that?" Mrs. Partin asked. "You just multiply the length by the width for each one," Tyra shared.

Their task was to work with a partner to answer the following questions about the rectangular prism they had created.

1. Looking at the net, how many rectangles are there?

   What is the area of each rectangle?

   Find the total area of the rectangles on your net.

2. The formula for surface area of a rectangular prism is $2lw + 2lh + 2wh$. Show how you would find the surface area using the formula.

3. Which method did you think was easier? Why?

As pairs worked, Mrs. Partin moved through the room asking questions and clarifying ideas. One group was still confused about the number of rectangles (listing 4 instead of 6 because they did not count the 2 squares). Mrs. Partin asked the students several questions to clarify the characteristics of a rectangle and to help them see that the squares should be included in their count. Mrs. Partin found several pairs who struggled with the dimensions of some parts of the rectangular prism, and she began posing questions to help them see ways to use the known dimensions to find the unknown dimensions.

Students were asked to talk with partners to compare finding the surface area by looking at the net or using the formula, sharing the method they thought was easier. Mrs. Partin reminded them that there was no right or wrong answer. Abby shared, "I thought the net was easier because you can see it and won't make a mistake. There are too many formulas to remember." Alex said, "The formula is better. Just put the numbers in and it's less work. You don't have to add up as many."

Mrs. Partin summed up their ideas, stating that there were different ways to find the surface area and that knowing different methods could be helpful, adding that tomorrow they would be using what they knew to explore finding the surface area of triangular prisms.

About the Math

In this lesson students reviewed geometry ideas as they verbalized definitions and characteristics of rectangles and squares, compared the characteristics of rectangles and rectangular prisms, and practiced spatial visualization with nets. In addition, they were challenged to understand the concepts of area and surface area, work with the formula for determining surface area, and explore ways to find unknown data using known data from the nets.

The teacher encouraged partner talk throughout the lesson. While partners discussed ideas, she circulated through the room asking questions and requiring students to justify their ideas. She asked them to compare/contrast concepts (e.g., rectangle and rectangular prism, net and solid figure, formula and net as methods for determining surface area) to strengthen and assess their understanding of those concepts, and asked them to reflect on ways they solved the problem (e.g., what was easy or hard about the methods). Students communicated frequently, and in a variety of ways, as they explored the lesson ideas.

Communicating About Data and Probability

Students in grades 6 through 8 are using their understanding of probability to make and test conjectures as they conduct and analyze the results of experiments. They are learning to use various methods (e.g., lists and tree diagrams) to organize the data collected and are learning to compute probabilities based on those data. The following lesson challenged seventh-grade students to test their predictions, analyze their findings, and justify their decisions regarding the fairness of a probability game.

The Activity

Mrs. Alexander began the lesson by sharing the following probability activity with her students and asking them if it was a fair game.

> **Activity directions: There are 2 players and 1 number cube (with numbers 1 to 6). Player A scores a point if an even number is rolled, and player B scores a point if an odd number is rolled. Is it a fair game? Justify your answer.**

Mrs. Alexander asked students to turn to a partner and share their ideas, and then asked students to share ideas with the class. Jimmy explained, "It is fair. They have the same chance of winning!" Buddy added, "There are the same amount of odd and even numbers." Mrs. Alexander asked Jimmy and Buddy to give her more details to help her understand. Jimmy continued "2, 4, 6, are even and 1, 3, 5, are odd, so there are 3 of each." "What is a fair game?" Mrs. Alexander asked. Rita answered, "It's when the chances are the same for both people." Ellen added, "It's when the probability is the same." Mrs. Alexander continued to probe: "What is the probability that you would roll an even number?"

STUDENT: 3 out of 6
MRS. ALEXANDER: Can you say it any other way?
STUDENT: 50%
STUDENT: You could do it like a fraction, $\frac{3}{6}$.

STUDENT: Or $\frac{1}{2}$.

MRS. ALEXANDER: How can it be $\frac{1}{2}$ and $\frac{3}{6}$?

STUDENT: It's just like reducing the fraction.

MRS. ALEXANDER: So what is the probability that an odd number is rolled?

The students explained that it would be $\frac{1}{2}$, just like the probability for rolling an even number. Mrs. Alexander praised the students for using specific data (e.g., telling her the quantity of odd or even numbers on the number cube and expressing the probability of each outcome). She stressed that she would not have been convinced if they had simply said "It's fair because the probability is the same," but was convinced when she heard their specific data. Mrs. Alexander then modified the probability game and again asked students to decide with their partner if the new game was fair or unfair, reminding them to be ready to justify their answers.

> There are 2 players and 1 number cube (with numbers 1 to 6). Player A scores a point if the number is greater than 3, and player B scores a point if the number is less than 3. Is it a fair game? Justify your answer.

Students shared their decisions that the game was not fair, verbalizing the probabilities for each player. Again, Mrs. Alexander modified the game.

> There are 2 players and 1 number cube (with numbers 1 to 6). Player A scores a point if the number is a multiple of 2, and player B scores a point if the number is a multiple of 3. Is it a fair game? Justify your answer.

Again students talked to partners and shared their ideas with the class, justifying their decision (that the game was not fair) by stating the multiples of each number and determining the probability for each outcome.

Mrs. Alexander then gave each pair of students a game mat for a Probability Grand Prix game. Each student was given a game marker and a number cube, and Mrs. Alexander explained the directions. This time, they would actually play the game and then determine the fairness of the game. She explained that there were 2 players and 2 number cubes (each with numbers 1 to 6). Each player would get a number cube and they would roll them simultaneously and then find the product of the rolls (she asked them to clarify what that meant to ensure that they understood that they were to multiply the numbers rolled).

MRS. ALEXANDER: What is the smallest possible product?

STUDENT: 1 would be the smallest product because $1 \times 1 = 1$.

MRS. ALEXANDER: What is the greatest possible product?

STUDENT: $6 \times 6 = 36$, so 36 would be the greatest.

MRS. ALEXANDER: So the products could range from 1 to 36? Let's say that Player A moves one space on the game mat each time the product is 18 or less, and player B moves one space when the product is from 19 to 36. I wonder who will be first to the finish line? Does that sound like a fair game?

Many students nodded their heads and she told them to begin the game, asking them to think about fairness as they played the game.

As students played the probability game, Mrs. Alexander moved through the room observing them (see Figure 9–4). Charles looked frustrated that he rarely was able to move. Alice was excited to move quickly from space to space on the game mat. After the students completed the game, Mrs. Alexander again asked, "Is it a fair game?" and students shouted "No!" Mrs. Alexander asked all A players who had won the game to stand up, and many students stood up. Then, she asked all B players who had won the game to stand up, and no one stood up! Many of the students smiled and laughed, and Mrs. Alexander said, "Did you think it would be fair?" Mary said she did because "we split the number right down the middle". Others nodded. "So what happened? Why isn't this a fair game?" she asked. She asked students to work with partners to explain why the game was not fair, and reminded them of her love for specific data. "Please don't just tell me the chances weren't the same. I need to know why—get specific." The students got to work. Some began listing all of the possible products, others made tree diagrams to display the products, and still others created tables to show their data.

After reviewing the data he had collected about possible products, Marty began writing, but his response was very general (see Figure 9–5). Mrs. Alexander, who was circulating through the room observing students' work, prompted him to add more data to his justification so she would be convinced that his answer made sense.

Students represented their data in a variety of ways (see Figures 9–6 and 9–7). Brendan and Allison created tree diagrams. Jason and Katie listed all of the possible products. Mrs. Alexander asked both pairs to read their justifications to the class, highlighting the different but effective ways in which they justified their decision that

Figure 9–4 *Most students predicted a fair game but were surprised as they played the game with partners.*

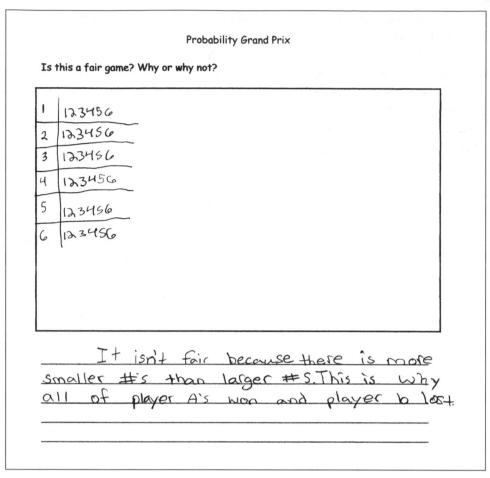

Probability Grand Prix

Is this a fair game? Why or why not?

1	123456
2	123456
3	123456
4	123456
5	123456
6	123456

It isn't fair because there is more smaller #'s than larger #S. This is why all of player A's won and player b lost.

Figure 9–5 *While this student correctly states that the game is not fair, his response lacks specific data and reasoning to prove his answer.*

the game was definitely not fair. For homework, she asked students to create a new version of the game that would be fair and to be sure they could justify its fairness.

About the Math

In this lesson, students were asked to determine the fairness of a probability game and to justify their decision. The class reviewed the concept of fair games and discussed ways to organize data in order to analyze the outcomes (e.g., lists and tree diagrams).

The lesson included a writing task that required students to justify their answers. Prior to the task, the teacher reinforced key points for writing to justify (e.g., the use of specific data). The partner work allowed students to hear others' ideas and test their own ideas prior to the writing task. And the student writing samples provided the teacher with insight into their level of understanding of the probability concepts, as well as their ability to effectively justify their answers.

Probability Grand Prix

Is this a fair game? Why or why not?

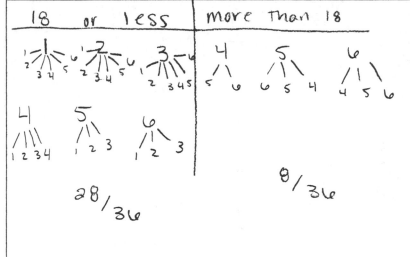

18 or less	more than 18

28/36

8/36

In the game, player A has
a 28/36 chance of moving a
space, and player B has a 8/36
chance of moving. The tree diagram
shows all the possible out comes
of 18 or less compared to more
than 18. Clearly, player A has a higher
probibility of winning the game.
Its not a fair game because the
probibility isnt the same for each
player.

Figure 9–6 *The tree diagram effectively displays the possible outcomes and the
students use the data to justify their decision that the game is not fair.*

Probability Grand Prix

Is this a fair game? Why or why not?

$1 \cdot 1 = 1$	$3 \cdot 1 = 3$	$5 \cdot 1 = 5$
$1 \cdot 2 = 2$	$3 \cdot 2 = 6$	$5 \cdot 2 = 10$
$1 \cdot 3 = 3$	$3 \cdot 3 = 9$	$5 \cdot 3 = 15$
$1 \cdot 4 = 4$	$3 \cdot 4 = 12$	$5 \cdot 4 = 20$
$1 \cdot 5 = 5$	$3 \cdot 5 = 15$	$5 \cdot 5 = 25$
$1 \cdot 6 = 6$	$3 \cdot 6 = 18$	$5 \cdot 6 = 36$
	$4 \cdot 1 = 4$	$6 \cdot 1 = 6$
$2 \cdot 1 = 2$	$4 \cdot 2 = 8$	$6 \cdot 2 = 12$
$2 \cdot 2 = 4$	$4 \cdot 3 = 12$	$6 \cdot 3 = 18$
$2 \cdot 3 = 6$	$4 \cdot 4 = 16$	$6 \cdot 4 = 24$
$2 \cdot 4 = 8$	$4 \cdot 5 = 20$	$6 \cdot 5 = 30$
$2 \cdot 5 = 10$	$4 \cdot 6 = 24$	$6 \cdot 6 = 36$
$2 \cdot 6 = 12$		

$\frac{7}{9}$ A   B $\frac{2}{9}$

28   8

winning outcomes   winning outcomes

The game is not fair. If either die gets
1, 2, or 3, then the answer is automatically
≤ 18. $4 \cdot 4$ is also less than 18.

Figure 9–7 *These students record the possible outcomes in a list and share their insights after reviewing their data.*

Linking Communication and Math Content

Communication provides students with opportunities to explore math content and expand their understanding of that content. Whether lessons focus on numbers and operations, algebra, geometry, measurement, or data and probability, students benefit from ongoing opportunities to talk and write about their ideas. When lessons are carefully selected, they serve to expand and refine students' communication skills as well as their understanding of math content.

Questions for Discussion

1. How are communication skills reinforced during these math lessons?

2. Do these lessons show examples of communication as a vehicle for exploring math ideas and communication as a means of expressing math ideas? List some examples of each. Do any activities illustrate both?

3. In what ways do the teachers support students as they talk and write about math?

4. How do the teachers support struggling students and challenge more able students during these activities?

A Challenge to Educators

What students learn—about particular concepts and procedures as well as about thinking mathematically—depends on the ways in which they engage in mathematical activity in their classrooms.

—National Council of Teachers of Mathematics,
Professional Standards for Teaching Mathematics

In mathematics, as in other subject areas, communication is a critical process through which students develop content understanding. Talking and writing about math helps students test their thinking, clarify misunderstandings, discover alternate ideas, and develop conceptual understanding. As students express their thoughts and listen to their own thinking, they often recognize their own confusions, question their own understanding, and work to modify and refine their thinking.

Communication about math also plays a critical role in our assessment process. Communication, whether oral or written, makes our students' thinking visible. It provides us with more information than just a "right" or "wrong" answer, allowing us to assess the degree to which our students understand a skill or concept. Communication is the lens through which we can see our students' thoughts.

While we certainly agree that communicating about content is valuable for both learning and assessing that content, communicating about math offers special challenges for our students. In mathematics, the communication process is complicated by a specialized vocabulary, an uncertainty about how to verbalize one's thinking, and the sheer complexity of some math concepts.

We can assist students in developing their math communication skills by paying attention to vocabulary development, using teacher questioning techniques that spark student thinking, and modeling ways to express mathematical ideas. Opportunities to talk about math through cooperative learning activities and write about math through a variety of classroom writing assignments assist students in developing their communication skills. In addition, frequent and specific feedback helps students refine and enhance their communication skills. As we explore best practices in communicating about mathematics, it is important to keep in mind that it is the combination of effective communication skills and an understanding of math concepts that leads to well-developed writing and thorough and insightful discussions about math.

Our Challenge

Our challenge as teachers is to learn ways to routinely incorporate communication into our math instruction. While maintaining our focus on content standards, we must also expand our thinking to consider how students will best learn that content. Through the process of communication, as well as the other NCTM process standards, we are providing students with opportunities to explore, refine, and express their content understanding. Communication must become an essential part of our students' math experiences.

As the complexity of math increases, students' difficulty talking and writing about it increases, challenging us to strengthen our repertoire of support strategies. Developing our questioning skills and our understanding of writing processes will help us better support our students. Opening dialogues with reading and language arts specialists may provide us with additional skills and strategies to apply to our math teaching.

We must find ways to stimulate meaningful talk and writing in our classrooms. Students need something to talk about. By posing thoughtful questions, creating engaging problem tasks, or utilizing the excitement of math-related literature or real-world data, we can stimulate conversations about critical math topics. Planning with colleagues and sharing lesson ideas provides us with support in designing these tasks.

We must use communication to foster reflection about our students and our teaching. We must analyze students' talk and writing in order to better understand their thinking. Rather than be concerned primarily with correctness, we must shift our focus to assessing and developing knowledge and skills. And we must find ways to use students' communication to inform and change our own teaching. We must accept some responsibility for the communication we hear and see and consider how changes in our teaching might improve student learning.

Communication is a key to learning in any content area. In mathematics we face the additional challenges of a technical language, a complex content, and traditional ideas about how it should be taught. But recognizing the critical role of communication in building content understanding will motivate us to accept the challenge of integrating it into our classroom practices. Communication brings enthusiasm and fun into our math classrooms. It allows us to hear our students' ideas and marvel at their insights. It moves math from a rote activity to a thinking skill, and stimulates students to develop and share mathematical reasoning. It allows us to hear each student's thoughts and provides a tool through which we can support each one in developing his or her own understanding. Communication is an invaluable tool for developing math understanding.

CLASSROOM-TESTED TIP

Reflecting on Our Instructional Practices

Our goal, as teachers, is to continue to strengthen our instructional skills to meet the changing needs of our students. Although communicating about mathematics may not have been a critical part of our own experiences as students, we recognize its power to enhance our math instruction and help our students better understand math ideas. We are challenged to alter the traditional drill-and-practice style of math instruction and to find ways to integrate communication into our daily lessons. Try these activities to continue to refine your teaching skills:

- Read a piece of professional literature about writing and mathematics and reflect on it as you think about your own experiences in the classroom. See the Resources to Support Teachers section at the end of the book for possible titles.

- Listen to your students and look carefully at their writing. Look for evidence of what they know and clues for how you can help them improve both their math and communication skills.

- Try new techniques and activities and then reflect on what you've tried. You might model the writing of class summaries or do a think-aloud to demonstrate writing to justify an answer. If your techniques are not immediately successful, modify them, or your delivery of them, to find the best approach for your students.

- Find a colleague with whom you can discuss ideas, share experiences, or even observe his or her teaching.

- When planning math lessons, consider ways to incorporate communication activities related to all content standards. Include a variety of talking and writing activities that will support your students' understanding of the math content.

Questions for Discussion

1. How might you ensure that communication is integrated into your math teaching?

2. How might you improve your own skills at helping students communicate about math?

3. How might you collaborate with colleagues to discuss and expand your understanding of the skills involved in communicating about mathematics?

Additional Resources for Communication

The following resources are meant to support you as you continue to explore the communication standard in grades 6 through 8. You will find a variety of text resources—books that will provide you with additional communication activities or instructional strategies. A list of math websites is included to supply you with classroom tasks, electronic manipulative ideas, or teacher resources. And for additional professional development, several video products are listed which allow you to view math communication in classrooms and reflect on the video lessons whether alone or with a group of your colleagues.

Text Resources

The following text resources provide a variety of activities and strategies for supporting students as they develop their communication skills.

Burns, M. 1995. *Writing in Math Class—A Resource for Grades 2–8*. Sausalito, CA: Math Solutions.

Chapin, S., C. O'Connor, and N. Canavan Anderson. 2003. *Classroom Discussions: Using Math Talk to Help Students Learn*. Sausalito, CA: Math Solutions.

Countryman, J. 1992. *Writing to Learn Mathematics*. Portsmouth, NH: Heinemann.

Kagan, S. 1992. *Cooperative Learning*. San Clemente, CA: Resources for Teachers.

Murray, M. 2004. *Teaching Mathematics Vocabulary in Context*. Portsmouth, NH: Heinemann.

National Council of Teachers of Mathematics. 1989. *Curriculum and Evaluation Standards for School Mathematics*. Reston, VA: Author.

———. 1991. *Professional Standards for Teaching Mathematics*. Reston, VA: Author.

———. 1995. *Assessment Standards for School Mathematics*. Reston, VA: Author.

———. 2000. *Principles and Standards for School Mathematics*. Reston, VA: Author.

_____. 2006. *Curriculum Focal Points for Prekindergarten through Grade 8 Mathematics.* Reston, VA: Author.

O'Connell, S. 2001a. *Math—The Write Way for Grades 6–7.* Columbus, OH: Frank Schaffer Publications.

_____. 2005. *Now I Get It: Strategies for Building Confident and Competent Mathematicians K–6.* Portsmouth, NH: Heinemann.

Rothstein, A., E. Rothstein, and G. Lauber. 2007. *Write for Mathematics.* Thousand Oaks, CA: Corwin Press.

Whitin, P., and D. Whitin. 2000. *Math Is Language Too: Talking and Writing in the Mathematics Classroom.* Urbana, IL: National Council of Teachers of English.

Zikes, D. 2003. *Big Book of Math K–6.* San Antonio, TX: Dinah-Might Adventures.

Web Resources

The following websites provide a variety of lesson ideas, classroom resources, and ready-to-use math communication tasks.

www.abcteach.com/directory/basics/math/problem_solving
The problem-solving activities on this abcteach website provide opportunities for talk and writing about math.

www.eduplace.com
This Houghton Mifflin website contains brain teasers for grades 3 through 8 as well as an archive of past problems.

www.etacuisenaire.com
This is the website of the ETA/Cuisenaire Company, which is a supplier of classroom mathematics manipulatives and teacher resource materials.

www.heinemann.com
This website of Heinemann Publishing provides a variety of professional development resources for teachers.

www.illuminations.nctm.org
Explore a variety of communication activities on this website of the National Council of Teachers of Mathematics.

www.learner.org/channel/courses/teachingmath/grades6_8/session_02/index.html
This Annenberg Media site offers a free, self-paced online course to help teachers better understand the communication standard, including lesson excerpts, video clips, and reflection questions.

www.math.com/teachers.html
This site offers lesson plans, classroom resources, links to "free stuff," problems of the week, and online tutorial assistance.

www.mathforum.org
This website has a problem of the week component that offers feedback from mentors on problem-solving and communication skills. There is a fee to subscribe.

www.mathleague.com/help/help.htm
This Math League website supports students in grades 4 through 8 with explanations, examples, and some illustrations for key math concepts across the content standards.

www.nctm.org
> On this website of the National Council of Teachers of Mathematics (NCTM) you will find information on regional and national conferences sponsored by NCTM, as well as a variety of professional development materials.

www.nlvm.usu.edu/en/nav/vlibrary.html
> The National Library of Virtual Manipulatives offers a free collection of virtual manipulatives to help teachers demonstrate math concepts or to allow students in grades PK–12 to explore math concepts.

www.puzzlemaker.com
> Create crossword puzzles and word searches for key math vocabulary using this website.

www.wits.ac.za/ssproule/pow.htm
> This website lists links to problem-of-the-week sites at all academic levels and includes a site rating system. The problems provide opportunities to get students communicating about math ideas.

Staff Development Training Videos

The following professional development training videos feature lessons that incorporate communication as a fundamental component and offer tips and strategies for helping students communicate effectively about mathematics. These video programs allow teachers to view classroom lessons and include manuals with reflection questions and activity ideas.

Burns, M. 1989. *Mathematics for Middle School*. Vernon Hills, IL: ETA Cuisenaire.
Using Writing to Strengthen Your Students' Understanding of Math Concepts and Skills, Grades 3–6. 2005. Bellevue, WA: Bureau of Education and Research.

REFERENCES

Andrini, B. 1991. *Cooperative Learning and Mathematics*. San Juan Capistrano, CA: Resources for Teachers, Inc.

Anno, M., and M. Anno. 1983. *Anno's Mysterious Multiplying Jar*. New York: Philomel Books.

Burns, M. 1995. *Writing in Math Class*. Sausalito, CA: Math Solutions.

Chambers, D., ed. 2002. *Putting Research into Practice in the Elementary Grades*. Reston, VA: National Council of Teachers of Mathematics.

Corwin, R. B. 1996. *Talking Mathematics: Supporting Children's Voic*es. Portsmouth, NH: Heinemann.

Countryman, J. 1992. *Writing to Learn Mathematics*. Portsmouth, NH: Heinemann.

Kagan, S. 1992. *Cooperative Learning*. San Clemente, CA: Resources for Teachers.

Kilpatrick, J., W. G. Martin, and D. Schifter, eds. 2003. *A Research Companion to Principles and Standards for School Mathematics*. Reston, VA: National Council of Teachers of Mathematics.

Marzano, R., D. Pickering, and J. Pollock. 2001. *Classroom Instruction That Works: Research-Based Strategies for Increasing Student Achievement*. Reston, VA: Association for Supervision and Curriculum Development.

Moore, D. W., S. A. Moore, P. M. Cunningham, and J. W. Cunningham. 1994. *Developing Readers and Writers in the Content Areas K–12*. White Plains, NY: Longman.

Murray, M. 2004. *Teaching Mathematics Vocabulary in Context*. Portsmouth, NH: Heinemann.

Nagda, A. Whitehead. 2000. *Tiger Math*. New York: Henry Holt and Company.

National Council of Teachers of Mathematics. 1989. *Curriculum and Evaluation Standards for School Mathematics*. Reston, VA: Author.

———. 1991. *Professional Standards for Teaching Mathematics*. Reston, VA: Author.

———. 1995. *Assessment Standards for School Mathematics*. Reston, VA: Author.

———. 2000. *Principles and Standards for School Mathematics*. Reston, VA: Author.

Neuschwander, C. 1997. *Sir Cumference and the First Round Table*. Watertown, MA: Charlesbridge Publishing.

O'Connell, S. R. 2001. *Math—The Write Way for Grades 6–7*. Columbus, OH: Frank Schaffer Publications.

———. 2005. *Now I Get It: Strategies for Building Confident and Competent Mathematicians K–6*. Portsmouth, NH: Heinemann.

Schwartz, D. 1985. *How Much Is a Million?* New York: Lee & Shepard Books.

Scieszka, J., and L. Smith. 1995. *Math Curse.* New York: Viking.

Stenmark, J. K., ed. 1991. *Mathematics Assessment—Myths, Models, Good Questions, and Practical Suggestions.* Reston, VA: National Council of Teachers of Mathematics.

Van de Walle, J. A. 2004. *Elementary and Middle School Mathematics: Teaching Developmentally.* New York: Pearson.

Whitin, P., and D. Whitin. 2000. *Math Is Language Too: Talking and Writing in the Mathematics Classroom.* Urbana, IL: National Council of Teachers of English.

Why Are Student Activities on a CD?

At first glance, the CD included with this book appears to be a collection of teaching tools and student activities, much like the activities that appear in many teacher resource books. But rather than taking a book to the copier to copy an activity, the CD allows you to simply print off the desired page on your home or work computer. No more standing in line at the copier or struggling to carefully position the book on the copier so you can make a clean copy. And with our busy schedules, we appreciate having activities that are classroom ready and aligned with our math standards.

The editing feature of the CD allows you to modify each activity to suit the needs, interests, and skill level of your students. With this CD, you are able to use the activities exactly as they appear in the book or to modify them in countless ways. You may want to simplify some tasks or add complexity to others. The activities often include several parts or have added challenge extensions. When it is appropriate for your students, simply delete these sections for a quick way to simplify or shorten the tasks. Here are some examples of ways you may want to change the tasks and why. A more complete version of this guide with additional samples for editing the activities can be found on the CD-ROM.

Editing the CD to Motivate and Engage Students

Personalizing Tasks or Capitalizing on Students' Interests

The editable CD provides a quick and easy way to personalize math problems. Substituting students' names, the teacher's name, a favorite restaurant, sports team, or location can immediately engage students. You know the interests of your students. Mentioning their interests in your problems is a great way to increase their enthusiasm for the activities. Think about their favorite activities and simply substitute their interests for those that might appear in the CD tasks.

In the second version of the following task, the teacher knows that many of his students have never belonged to a swim team, so he modifies the task to fit their interest in track, a popular sport at the school. Using the editable CD feature, he makes simple changes to the problem task to create a version of the problem that works well for his students.

Note: This type of editing is important when the problem situation may not be culturally appropriate for your students. It may be that they have no previous experience with swim clubs or swim teams and would not relate to this prompt. Substituting an experience that makes sense for your students will make the problem relevant to them.

Name _____

Swimming Laps

The swim team was practicing laps in a 75-meter pool. Ben swam $\frac{5}{8}$ of the way, while Kyle swam 60% of the distance, and Alex made it .65 of the distance.

1. How far did each boy swim?

Ben _____   Kyle _____   Alex _____

Show your work.

2. Which boy swam the farthest? Use math data to prove your answer. _____

Show your work.

_____
_____
_____
_____

Challenge: The swim coach told the boys that they had to double the distance they swam. How far will they have to swim? Explain how you got your answer.

May be copied for classroom use. © 2008 by Susan O'Connell and Suzanne Croskey from *Introduction to Communication: Grades 6–8* (Heinemann: Portsmouth, NH).

Name _____

Running Laps

The track team was practicing running laps on a 400-meter track. Ben ran $\frac{5}{8}$ of the way, while Kyle ran 60% of the distance, and Alex made it .65 of the distance.

1. How far did each boy run?

Ben _____   Kyle _____   Alex _____

Show your work.

2. Which boy ran the farthest? Use math data to prove your answer. _____

Show your work.

_____
_____
_____
_____

Challenge: The track coach told the boys that they had to double the distance they ran. How far will they have to run? Explain how you got your answer.

May be copied for classroom use. © 2008 by Susan O'Connell and Suzanne Croskey from *Introduction to Communication: Grades 6–8* (Heinemann: Portsmouth, NH).

Editing the CD to Differentiate Instruction

Modifying the Readability of Tasks

Adding some fun details can generate interest and excitement in story problems, but you might prefer to modify some problems for students with limited reading ability. While the problems in the second version that follow are the same as in the first version, the tasks are written in simpler ways to support those students who might benefit from fewer words and simpler vocabulary. Simply deleting some of the words on the editable form will result in an easy-to-read version of the same task.

Name _____

Which Phone?

Joe's parents have told him that they will buy him a cell phone if he compares the cost of the plans so that he can get the best buy.

Talk Time offers a plan for 29.95 per month and $.25 for each minute.

Cell to Cell offers a plan that is $19.95 per month and $.50 for each minute.

1. Describe several methods Joe could use to compare the prices in the plans.

_____

_____

_____

_____

_____

_____

2. Complete the table for each phone company to compare the total cost for the following numbers of minutes: 5, 10, 25, 50, 75.

Talk Time		Cell to Cell	
Minutes	Total Cost	Minutes	Total Cost
5		5	
10		10	
25		25	
50		50	
75		75	

3. Write an equation to show how you found the total cost. Let *m* represent the number of minutes.

Talk Time: _____

Cell to Cell: _____

Name _____

Which Phone?

Joe is buying a cell phone. Which plan should he buy?

- Talk Time: $29.95 per month and $.25 for each minute.
- Cell to Cell: $19.95 per month and $.50 for each minute.

1. How could Joe compare the prices in the plans? Describe a few ways.

_____

_____

_____

_____

_____

2. Complete the table to compare the cost for 5, 10, 25, 50, and 75 minutes of phone time.

Talk Time		Cell to Cell	
Minutes	Total Cost	Minutes	Total Cost
5		5	
10		10	
25		25	
50		50	
75		75	

3. Write an equation to show how you found the total cost. Let *m* represent the number of minutes.

Talk Time: _____

Cell to Cell: _____

Creating Shortened or Tiered Tasks

While many students are able to move from one task to another, some students benefit from focusing on one task at a time. By simply separating parts of a task, either by cutting the page into two parts or by using the editable CD feature to put the parts of the task on separate pages, teachers can help focus students on the first part of the task before moving them to the second part. Teachers might choose to provide all students with the first part and then give students the second part after they have completed the first part and had their work checked by the teacher. In this sample, the two parts of the task initially appeared on the same page. In the modified version shown here, the two parts of the task are separated and the work box and lines for writing responses are enlarged for students who may need more writing or work space.

Name _____

Puzzling Measurements

Jason is shopping for ingredients to make punch. Before he can buy them, he has to figure out how to change the units on his recipe to match the units on the ingredient containers. Can you help him out?

The recipe calls for 2 gallons of lemonade, but it is sold in pints. How many pints are in 2 gallons?

_____

Show your work.

Explain how you know.

_____
_____
_____
_____
_____
_____

May be copied for classroom use. © 2008 by Susan O'Connell and Suzanne Croskey from *Introduction to Communication: Grades 6–8* (Heinemann: Portsmouth, NH).

Name _____

More Puzzling Measurements

Jason 's punch recipe calls for 4 quarts of lemon-lime soda, but Jason only has a 1-cup measuring cup. How many cups of soda are in 4 quarts?

Show your work.

Compare the measurement problems. What was similar about solving each problem?

_____
_____
_____

Challenge: Share a rule to explain the operation you use when converting from a smaller unit to a larger unit. Give an example to explain your thinking.

_____
_____
_____

May be copied for classroom use. © 2008 by Susan O'Connell and Suzanne Croskey from *Introduction to Communication: Grades 6–8* (Heinemann: Portsmouth, NH).

Modifying Data

While all students may work on the same problem task, modifying the problem data will allow teachers to create varying versions of the task. Using the editable forms, you can either simplify the data or insert more challenging data including larger numbers, integers, decimals, or percents.

In the second version that follows, the data were altered to create a problem with a bit more complexity. In the initial version the admission discount is 10%, but the modified version includes discounts of 15% and 20%. In addition, the students are asked to calculate the wait time when two people ride at a time. Whether you decide to simply change the numbers in the problem or slightly alter the other problem information, the editable feature of the CD will allow you to create various versions of the original activity.

Name _____

Adventure Park

1. To celebrate their 11th birthday, Dan and his twin sister Jan went with their mother and grandmother to Adventure Park. His grandmother was excited to get the senior discount. How much did they pay for admission?

_____

Admission Costs
Children (12 and under) - Half the adult admission
Adults - $8.50
Seniors - 10% off the adult admission

Show your work.

Explain how you got your answer.

_____
_____
_____

2. Dan got in line for the Horse Race Rodeo Ride. A rider was sent on a horse every 20 seconds. There were 15 people in front of Dan. How long did it take before it was Dan's turn to ride the horse? _____

Justify your answer.

_____
_____
_____

Challenge: Create a word problem using the amusement park admission data. Write the equation to match your word problem and solve your problem.

May be copied for classroom use. © 2008 by Susan O'Connell and Suzanne Croskey from *Introduction to Communication: Grades 6–8* (Heinemann: Portsmouth, NH).

Name _____

Adventure Park

1. To celebrate their 11th birthday, Dan and his twin sister Jan went with their mother and grandmother to Adventure Park. His grandmother was excited to get the senior discount. How much did they pay for admission?

_____

Admission Costs
Children (12 and under) - 20% off the adult admission
Adults - $8.60
Seniors - 15% off the adult admission

Show your work.

Explain how you got your answer.

_____
_____
_____

2. Dan got in line for the Horse Race Rodeo Ride. A rider was sent on a horse every 25 seconds. There are 15 people in front of Dan. How long did it take before it is Dan's turn to ride the horse? _____

Justify your answer.

_____
_____
_____

Challenge: Create a word problem using the amusement park admission data. Write the equation to match your word problem and solve your problem.

May be copied for classroom use. © 2008 by Susan O'Connell and Suzanne Croskey from *Introduction to Communication: Grades 6–8* (Heinemann: Portsmouth, NH).